Dominican Republic

Sarah Cameron

Contents

About the author

After taking a degree in Latin American Studies, Sarah Cameron has been travelling and writing on the continent, both as an economist and as an author for Footprint. Initially moonlighting for the *South American Handbook* while working for a British bank, in 1990 she parted company with the world of finance and has been contributing to the expansion of Footprint titles ever since. Sarah now concentrates solely on the Caribbean and is the author of *Footprint Caribbean Islands* as well as individual island titles such as Cuba, Barbados, St Lucia, Antigua and the Leeward Islands. When she is not travelling around the Caribbean sampling beaches and rum cocktails, she retreats to her 17th-century farmhouse in rural Suffolk.

Acknowledgements

Sarah Cameron would like to thank Sabrina Cambiaso in London and all the staff at the tourist office in Santo Domingo for their help in arranging research trips and for the provision of transport and accommodation all round the country. In addition, thanks go to a number of people who have given invaluable help with the text, including Griselda González in Santo Domingo, Joseba Egia of Iguana Mama for information on the north coast, Richard Weber of Tours, Trips, Treks and Travel for help with the southwest and the mountains, Urs and Mara Zumbuehl of Sunshine Services for updates on the Samaná peninsula and Joanne Keefer of Sam's Bar and Grill in Puerto Plata. Sarah is also grateful to Simone Bandle-Enslin, Ecoturismo, Subsecretaría de Areas Protegidas y Biodiversidad, for checking the text of the national parks. Others who have provided specialist help over the years for Footprint's coverage of the Dominican Republic include James Ferguson, Tricia Thorndike de Suriel, Omar and Estela Rodríguez, Kim Beddall, Robert Williams, Val Fraser and Dania Goris.

The Dominican Republic is one of the most diverse countries in the Caribbean and really does have something for everyone. You can laze on the beach under swaying palm trees with the blue sea lapping at your toes and sip rum cocktails while you catch up on your reading; or you can don a wet suit and tackle the rapids down rushing mountain rivers, leap off waterfalls, hike up the highest mountain in the Caribbean, cycle the country tracks and try your hand at any number of the other action-packed sports on offer. When you've tired of that, there are plenty of historical sites to investigate stretching back for centuries. In addition to Spanish colonial buildings, there are Taíno archaeological sites and cave drawings dating from well before Columbus set foot on the island, declaring it to be the most beautiful he had ever seen. Wherever you go, to the beaches, cities or mountains, you won't be far from the rhythm of merengue, the Latin music born in the Republic with an African soul.

Fiesta frolics

Dominicans are Spanish speaking and Roman Catholic, but their music and rhythms and the way in which they interpret their religion owe a huge debt to the African slaves brought here in colonial times to work at the sugar plantations and ranches. Their culture is overwhelmingly Latin, with African and American influences, but there is still a romantic attachment to the noble Indian and many Taíno names remain. The legacy of many races and faiths introduced into the Spanish colonial mould has produced some spectacular festivals, particularly the pre-Lenten Carnival, which stretches over several weeks. Parades are bursting with ingenuity and spontaneity within a framework of legends handed down for many generations. Each town has a variation on the carnival theme, with the devil represented by the piglet in Santiago, the bulls in Monte Cristi and fantastic and elaborate masks in La Vega. Dominicans also celebrate the Catholic feasts, with each town having its own saint's day, known as *patronales*. These usually involve the statue of the saint being paraded through the streets accompanied by an incoherent brass band, before being returned to the church for religious services. Meanwhile the town centre fills with market stalls and open-air stages for concerts. At fiesta time the rum flows, the band strikes up and everyone hits the dance floor. Merengue and the slower *bachata* are the local dances, but you will see and hear other Latin styles too, such as salsa.

Baseball mania

A baseball match is another time to see Dominicans in party mood. Join the crowds heading for the stadium and feel the excitement, helped along by beer, rum and the beat of drums. Sport and music are the two activities guaranteed to get Dominicans going. Rivalry between teams is intense but generally good natured, and there is intense pride that so many Dominican players are playing for millions of dollars in the USA.

At a glance

Santo Domingo

The colonial zone of the capital is a World Heritage Site and a prime example of Spanish colonial architecture from the first half of the 16th century. Pirates, earthquakes and hurricanes have taken their toll on the city, but recent renovation has restored much of its former glory. Delightful boutique hotels, gourmet restaurants and trendy bars and clubs now occupy many of the old mansions, alongside the fortresses and palaces housing museums. The modern city encircles the old, stretching along the coast east and west, and inland along the river bank heading north. Shanty towns have been cleared to make way for US-style shopping malls, supermarkets, banks and offices; but slum areas remain and cannot be forgotten, relics of the mass migration from the countryside to the city in the 20th century.

North to Santiago

The Autopista Duarte carries traffic from the capital to the second city of the Republic alongside the massive Cordillera Central containing the highest mountain in the Caribbean and extensive areas of national parks. This is an area of outstanding beauty, with forests, rivers and valleys providing unlimited opportunities for hiking, river sports, cycling, horse riding and other activities. Up in the hills, Constanza and Jarabacoa are the two small towns where you can find decent, rustic accommodation from which to set out on an adventure.

The North Coast

The sea is still sparkling with silver as it was when Columbus named Puerto Plata, now the main city on the north coast; the bays and beaches are still enticing visitors but with rather more peaceful intentions than the *conquistadores*. Beautiful scenery adorns this area, with the green mountains of the Cordillera

Septentrional tumbling down to the golden sand. Some fabulous golf courses have been built along the cliffs and there are comfortable beach resorts to go with them. A feature of the north coast, however, is the number of pleasant small hotels in or around friendly towns and villages like Sosúa and Cabarete. These are places overflowing with watersports opportunities, from diving in Sosúa to windsurfing and kiteboarding in Cabarete. A vibrant nightlife goes with the lifestyle and there are seaside bars, discos and casinos to suit all tastes.

Samaná Peninsula
For three months of the year, Samaná Bay is home to magnificent humpback whales that come here to mate and give birth. For many people this is the only reason they travel to the peninsula, as it is one of the best places in the world for whale watching. However, for several years now, the beaches of Las Terrenas and Las Galeras have been attracting Europeans and French Canadians. They came for the peace and quiet, and many stayed on to run small businesses such as guesthouses and restaurants. More recently there has been a mini-boom in tourism and lots of new hotels have been built, but they are all small and intimate, appealing to a range of budgets. It is a relaxing place with a spectacularly beautiful landscape of green hills, waterfalls, looming headlands and cliffs and miles of coconut palms along the flatter seashore.

The Southeast
This is the major area of tourist development, with large-scale resorts, most of which are all-inclusive. The international airports here receive more passengers than anywhere else in the country, lured by miles of white sand beaches, shaded by the archetypal coconut palms. For a beach holiday you can't go far wrong, with scuba diving and plenty of water toys to enliven the day-time activities. The resorts close to Santo Domingo, such as Boca Chica and Juan Dolio, offer the possibility of excursions to the capital for

sightseeing, and there are independent bars and restaurants to while away the after-dark hours. However, if you are at Bávaro or Punta Cana, you will be too remote for many day trips to see the rest of the country and there are very few places to eat and drink outside your hotel.

The Southwest
The least developed part of the island, the national parks of the arid southwest protect rare and endemic species of fauna and flora. Birdwatching is excellent and there are great opportunities for getting close to nature. Access problems have meant that some fabulous beaches are completely untouched and you are unlikely to see another tourist. The excessively saline Lago Enriquillo, below sea level, is home to iguanas, flamingos and crocodiles. Accommodation is limited and there are few places to eat, but this is off-the-beaten-track travel and the remoteness of the area is part of its attraction.

Trip planner

This is a tropical island in the sun, where you can expect hot, sunny days and warm, balmy nights, but you can be lucky or unlucky with the weather at any time of year. The dry season is traditionally December to May, but the climate is changing worldwide and there is no guarantee that the dry season will be dry, nor that the rainy season will be wet. The temperature averages a comfortable 25° C and there is not much seasonal variation, but humidity levels vary. Hurricane season is technically June to November, but two-thirds of hurricanes hit the island in September. Even in winter, which is supposed to be the dry season, the northern parts of the island can be affected by cold fronts moving down from the North American continent; these often bring heavy rain, grey skies and squally northern winds.

You might like to arrange a trip to coincide with an event, rather than a season. At the beginning of the year, the main religious festival is on 21 January, the day of the Virgen de la Altagracia; whale watching is from January to March; and Carnival is in February. At Easter all the Dominicans go on holiday, mostly to the beach, so get hotel bookings in early as everywhere is packed. June is the month for windsurfers and kiteboarders, when international competitions are held in Cabarete, while July is good for music lovers with the Santo Domingo Merengue Festival. If baseball is your sport – and it certainly fires up Dominicans – you can catch a game during the season in October to December, or during the *Serie Final* in January.

A weekend

If you have only a weekend to spend on the island, you might like to concentrate on the capital. Stroll around the sights of the colonial zone on the first day, take in a bar with live music or a nightclub after a meal at a good restaurant and maybe take a trip out to the beach at Boca Chica on the second day. Here you can wallow in turquoise water as clear and calm as a swimming pool, eat fried fish and *yaniqueques* for lunch and partake of some ice-cold beer, in the company of Dominican families out from the capital for a Sunday treat.

A week

A week's stay will allow you time on the beach and inland. If you fly to Puerto Plata you can combine a few days in Sosúa, relaxing and maybe taking a diving or snorkelling excursion along the coast, with a few days in Jarabacoa in the mountains. A more physically active beach spot is Cabarete, where you can spend time windsurfing or kiteboarding as well as cycling, but both places have good bars, restaurants and nightlife and you'll never be short of friends to party with. Jarabacoa can in fact be reached as a day trip from the coast if you just want to do a spot of whitewater rafting, but to hike Pico Duarte you will need a minimum of two days.

If you fly to Santo Domingo you can combine sightseeing in the capital with a trip to the mountains, or transfer to the Samaná peninsula by bus or small plane for an idyllic beach retreat. While there you can go whale watching or visit the Parque Nacional de los Haitises, just a couple of options among many excursions on offer.

Two weeks or more

Two weeks is of course a more attractive option, giving you time to see most of the country at a leisurely pace. If you want to see the west of the Republic it is best to fly to Santo Domingo and use the capital as a base, travelling to the west and back and then to the north coast and the mountains. The west offers a different perspective on Dominican life: the pace is slower, it is more remote and less Americanized and there are fewer facilities for tourists. If you have time, Constanza is a worthwhile place to visit in the mountains for its hikes to forests, rivers and waterfalls in national parks, and is a good combination with Jarabacoa for scenery, fresh air and wholesome food.

In a country with 55,000 hotel rooms and over two million tourists a year, there are some areas you may wish to avoid. The largest accumulation of hotels, mostly all-inclusive, is in Punta Cana and Bávaro in the east, followed by Juan Dolio, Bayahibe and Playa Dorada. Punta Cana and Bávaro are miles from anywhere and there are very few independent hotels and restaurants; visitors tend to come here to crash out on the beach and do little else. Juan Dolio and Bayahibe are within striking distance of Santo Domingo, and at least at the latter there are small hotels, cabañas and restaurants if you are on a budget. Playa Dorada is the most convenient resort area for visiting other parts of the country; it is within easy reach of Puerto Plata, Sosúa and Cabarete on the coast, and not far from the mountains if you want to explore inland.

Contemporary Dominican Republic

Dominicans are an outgoing, gregarious race who are used to living their lives outdoors on the street or in the fields. The warm, tropical climate encourages their sunny disposition, and they are always ready to strike up a conversation over a thimbleful of strong, black, sweet coffee or a bottle of the local Presidente beer. Some of the best music and entertainment takes place out of doors, usually along the seafront promenade, called the Malecón in all seaside towns, while merengue is the national passion and can be heard everywhere. Carnival is the epitome of expression in the Dominican Republic, an exuberant, colourful and raucous celebration of cultural history and present day concerns, with regional variations reflecting the diversity of the nation.

This diversity is perhaps most obviously reflected in the ethnicity of the Dominican people. African slaves began to arrive in Santo Domingo from the 1530s and formed an important part of the colonial population. From the mixing of Africans and Europeans emerged the coloured or mulatto population to which the majority of Dominicans nowadays belong. Successive governments tried to attract non-African settlers such as Canarian, Italian, Syrian and Japanese, especially after independence, when fears of Haitian territorial ambitions were at their highest and the 'whitening' of the population was deemed desirable. This racial policy is no longer on the agenda, but it shows how the country's leaders have traditionally viewed the nation as white, Hispanic and Christian.

Race and colour are still live issues. A whole vocabulary exists to describe skin colour and ethnic identity: most desirable, of course, is to be *blanco* (white), followed by *trigueño* (olive-skinned). Further down the hierarchy come *mulatto* and *moreno* (meaning dark or swarthy), and at the bottom is the term *negro*. Perhaps the most idiosyncratic racial category is that of the *indio*. The island's indigenous Taíno population was effectively extinct only 50 years after the arrival of the first European colonists. Yet the term is used to describe non-white Dominicans, and many identity cards describe their bearers as Indians, colour-coded as *oscuro* (dark), *quemado* (burnt), *canelo* (cinnamon) or *lavado* (washed). An *indio oscuro* may therefore be a dark-skinned individual of mixed ethnic background. Dominicans would far rather be known as a dark Indian than black, which might imply that they had Haitian ancestry. Recent research into DNA in the Dominican Republic and Puerto Rico has shown that claims of Taíno ancestry are not fanciful and that much of the population does indeed carry Amerindian genes passed down by enslaved Taína women before full-blooded Indians were wiped out.

The Dominican Republic is a relatively young democracy, having endured long and brutal dictatorships interspersed with US interventions. The most recent of these was the 31 years of repressive control by General Rafael Leonidas Trujillo. His assassination in 1961, with US help, brought a dark period of the country's history to a close, but created a power vacuum. Fear that the country was sliding into communism, like Cuba, resulted in a military coup. Civil war raged through the capital in 1965, provoking the USA to intervene, sending in 23,000 troops and installing a temporary government. The 1966 elections were won by Joaquín Balaguer, a former president and collaborator with Trujillo since 1930. With US aid and the help of a secret paramilitary force, La Banda, Balaguer succeeded in restoring some sort of order, strengthening the economy and maintaining an outward semblance of peace. Balaguer held power off and on for the rest of the century and was hugely influential even until his passing in 2002. The 2004 elections were free and fair and a new generation of politicians, unsullied by dictatorships, now competes at the ballot box.

There are still problems with the power structure, however, and political and economic reforms are badly needed. Corruption is endemic, the economy is in tatters, financial scandals in 2003 led to the closure of several banks, the repurchase of the privatized electricity companies was a disaster leading to power shortages and nationwide blackouts in 2004. Lack of confidence in the financial system brought a steep devaluation of the peso, with a consequent surge in prices which has not been reflected in wages. When it looked as though things couldn't get any worse and the IMF was making little headway in persuading the outgoing government to undertake fiscal reform, heavy rains hit the southwest in May 2004 and flooding killed hundreds. President Leonel Fernández, who took office for a second term in August 2004, faces an uphill struggle.

It is not all doom and despondency in the economy, as the devaluation has led to a boom in tourism. This industry is the largest foreign exchange earner, with annual receipts exceeding US$2 billion, but only 5% of the labour force is employed in tourism. Roughly half the population still lives in poverty, with a third lacking secure employment. Inequalities in national income are glaring and many depend on the informal economy to survive. Meanwhile, the rich live in the height of luxury and the oligarchy continues to dominate the economy.

The safety valve for this economic pressure is emigration, which began in the 1960s but accelerated in the troubled 1980s, and continues today as raging inflation forces people to seek a new life elsewhere. About one million legal and illegal Dominican immigrants live in the USA; the largest Latino group in the USA after Mexicans. Much of the money earned by migrants returns home in the form of regular payments to relatives left behind, valued at up to US$1 billion annually. These transfers provide a lifeline to many poor rural communities and those living in inner-city slums.

Despite the current economic crisis and an uncertain future, the Dominican people remain upbeat, positive and relaxed, testifying to their resilience. Their enjoyment of life is contagious and you cannot help but marvel at the exotic beauty of the island and the vibrancy of its diverse population.

Best

★ **Ten of the best**

1 **Colonial Santo Domingo** A World Heritage Site and an architectural feast for the eyes, with its well-preserved streets, fortresses, palaces and churches, p38.

2 **Jarabacoa** Feel the thrill of whitewater rafting, canyoning or any number of river sports, guaranteed to get the adrenaline pumping, p57.

3 **Pico Duarte** Hike the tallest mountain in the Caribbean, ascending through tropical rainforest and experiencing several different microclimates, p59.

4 **Mount Isabel de Torres** Take the cable car up from Puerto Plata for a magnificent view of the north coast, p68.

5 **Windsurfing at Cabarete** The best place in the Caribbean and one of the world's leading venues for windsurfing and kiteboarding, p73.

6 **Whale watching in Samaná Bay** Spot the humpback whales spouting and breaching during their annual migration to the warm Caribbean waters, p77.

7 **Take a break** in Boca Chica, one of the best places to find a beach bar and relax with a Presidente beer and a plate of *tostones*, p81.

8 **Altos de Chavón** A folly of the highest order, a mock-Italian artists' village with a church containing the ashes of Poland's patron saint, p85.

9 **Parque Nacional Isla Cabritos** Visit the fascinating Lago Enriquillo which is saltier than the sea and home to crocodiles, flamingos and iguanas, p102.

10 **Merengue** Swing your hips, step to the beat and dance with the Dominicans at the Carnival in Santo Domingo. Music is everywhere, p178.

The Dominican Republic is well served by scheduled and charter flights from Europe, North America, Latin America and the Caribbean. The main gateways are Santo Domingo, Puerto Plata, Santiago, La Romana and Punta Cana. Punta Cana and La Romana are only worth flying to if you are staying at one of the all-inclusive hotels along the eastern coast. If you want to start your travels on the south coast, including the capital, then fly to Santo Domingo. For the north coast use the airport outside Puerto Plata or Santiago. Most visitors arrive by air, although cruise ships call and there is a ferry from Puerto Rico. The Dominican Republic is connected by road to Haiti and there are frequent buses, but you are not allowed to take hired cars across the border. Public transport is varied and good value, with air-conditioned, long-distance buses connecting all the major towns, within and between which there are buses, minibuses and cars, known as *guaguas*, *conchos* and *carros públicos*. Car hire is readily available if you want to explore independently, and taxis will take you anywhere.

Getting there

Air

From Europe There are no direct scheduled flights to Santo Domingo from London. The main routes are via Paris with **Air France** (£558 to £688) or via Madrid with **Iberia** (£509 to £667) or **Air Europa** (£480 to £550). There are also flights from Amsterdam with **Martinair**, and Milan with **Lauda Air**. **Air Madrid** began flying from Madrid to Puerto Plata and Punta Cana in 2004, with initial summer fares of £399 and £429 respectively. **Martinair** flies to Puerto Plata from Amsterdam; **Condor** and/or **LTU** from Berlin, Düsseldorf, Frankfurt, Leipzig and Munich. In addition to scheduled flights there are hundreds of charters from many European cities.

From North America There are scheduled flights to Santo Domingo from Boston, Miami, New York and Philadelphia with **American Airlines**, **US Airways**, **Continental**, **Delta** and some smaller airlines. Puerto Plata receives **American Airlines** flights from Miami and New York. **Continental** also flies to Puerto Plata from New York. **Air Canada** flies from several Canadian cities to Puerto Plata and Punta Cana and there are many charter flights in high season. Santiago receives flights from **American Airlines** daily from Miami and New York, as well as **North American Airlines** and **Continental** from New York. In June 2004, **JetBlue**, a low-fare carrier, began flying from New York (JFK) to Santiago twice daily and to Santo Domingo daily with flights ranging from US$134 to US$299 each way when booked online. Further low-fare airlines, including **Spirit Airlines**, are scheduled to begin flying to Santo Domingo from Fort Lauderdale Hollywood International Airport in 2005.

From the Caribbean There are direct flights to Santo Domingo from Aruba, Barbados, Curaçao, Fort-de-France, Havana, Kingston, Mayagüez, Montego Bay, Pointe-à-Pitre, Port-au-Prince, Sint Maarten,

Airlines

Aeropostal www.aeropostal.com
Air Canada T 1-888-2472262 (Canada), www.aircanada.ca.
Air Europa T 0870-2401501 (UK), www.air-europa.com.
Air France T 0845-0845111 (UK), www.airfrance.com.
Air Jamaica Express T 020-85707999 (UK/Europe),
www.airjamaica.com.
Air Madrid T 0912-016010 (Spain), www.airmadrid.com.
American Airlines/American Eagle T 1-800-4337300 (North
America), www.aa.com.
Aserca www.asercaairlines.com
BWIA International T 0870-4992942 (UK/Europe),
www.bwee.com.
Condor T 0180-2337135 (Germany), www.condor.de.
Continental www.continental.com.
Copa www.copaair.com.
Cubana T 020-75377909 (UK), www.cubana.cu.
Delta Airlines T 1-800-2211212, www.delta.com.
Dominair T 800-528-2792
Dutch Caribbean Express www.flydce.com.
Iberia T 0845-6012854 (UK), www.iberia.com.
JetBlue T 1-800-5382583, www.jetblue.com.
Lauda Air www.lauda.it.
Liat T 1-268-4805625, www.liatairline.com.
LTU T 0211-9418333, www.ltu.com.
Martinair T 0206-011767 (Netherlands), www.martinair.com.
North American Airlines T 800-371-6297,
www.northamericanair.com.
Spirit Airlines www.spiritair.com
US Airways www.usairways.com.

For airline offices in the Dominican Republic, see Directory, p218.

→ Travel agents

Air Tours www.airtours.co.uk.
Caribbean World T 44-1208-5000011, www.firstcalltravel.com.
First Choice Tropical T 44-1293-588379, www.firstchoice.co.uk.
Journey Latin America T 44-20-87473108,
www.journeylatinamerica.co.uk.
South American Experience T 44-20-79765511,
www.southamericanexperience.co.uk.
Sportif Holidays/Dive Sportif T 44-1273-844919,
www.sportif-uk.com.
Thomas Cook T 44-1733-842266, www.thomascook.com.
Tropical Places T 44-1342-330744, www.tropicalplaces.co.uk.
Wholeworld Golf Travel T 44-20-87419987, www.golf.uk.com.
Wild Wings T 44-117-9375686, www.wildwings.co.uk.

San Juan and Santiago de Cuba. There are also many direct flights from around the Caribbean basin: **Copa** fly from Panama City, San José, Guatemala City and Managua; **Aserca** and **Aeropostal** fly from Caracas; **BWIA** fly from Trinidad with connections to other islands and countries, including the UK.

Regional flights to Puerto Plata include **TCI Sky King** from Providenciales and **American Eagle** from San Juan and Puerto Rico. **American Eagle** also flies to Santiago from San Juan and **Dominair** flies from Port-au-Prince.

Flights to Santo Domingo from Haiti include **Air Caribair**, around US$180 return and **Air Jamaica Express**.

Airport information
Aeropuerto Las Américas (SDQ), **T** 5490450/80, 23 km outside Santo Domingo, is clean and smart. Immediately on arrival there is a tourist office and an office selling tourist cards, see Travel Extras box, page 24. There is a bank and numerous car hire offices as you

come out of the customs hall, and an ATM in the departure area. If you drive into Santo Domingo you will need RD$15 for the toll (*peaje*). Leaving the airport on the ground floor, you will find the expensive, individual taxis. Upstairs, outside Departures, *colectivo* taxis cram up to six passengers into the vehicle, but are much cheaper; the drive to Santo Domingo should take around 30 minutes and cost no more than US$25. Alternatively, you can walk or take a *motoconcho* (motorcycle taxi) to the *autopista* (main road) for about US$2.50 and then catch a *guagua* (minibus) to Parque Enriquillo. If arriving late at night it may be better to go to Boca Chica (see page 81), about 10 km east of the airport, taxi about US$20.

From the capital to the airport for the return journey taxi prices range from US$15 to US$20. Most large hotels have a taxi service with set fares; various tour agencies also run minibuses to the airport. If you are travelling light, you can catch any bus to Boca Chica or towns east and get a *motoconcho* from the junction. On departure, the queue for check-in can be long and slow for large aircraft, so allow plenty of time. Departure tax is US$20. The departure area has a seating area, duty-free shops, cafés and burger restaurants.

The airport at Puerto Plata, **Gregorio Luperón International Airport** (POP), **T** 5860219/5860106, serves the entire north coast. It is 15-20 minutes from Puerto Plata, seven minutes from Sosúa and 20 minutes from Cabarete. If you are travelling light, you can walk out of the airport up to the junction and catch a bus passing along the main road to Sosúa and Cabarete or in the other direction to Puerto Plata. There is a small bank for foreign exchange (closed weekends), car hire agencies and a few shops. There is an airport at **Santiago** (STI), **T** 5824894, also serving the north coast.

! ● Remember there is a one-hour time difference between Haiti (GMT-5) and the Dominican Republic (GMT-4).

The airport at **Punta Cana** (PUJ), **T** 6868790, is busy with charter flights and most people who arrive here are on package holidays. The airport is in a remote area and there are no buses, so the only way to get to your hotel is by transfer bus or taxi.

La Romana airport (LRM), **T** 5565565, is small and compact, located just outside of the town, the other side of the road from the Casa de Campo resort. Buses pass on the road from La Romana to Bayahibe, or there are taxis.

The **El Portillo** airport (EPS), just east of Las Terrenas on the road to El Limón and Samaná, is currently the only airstrip with regular services to the Samaná peninsula. It is mostly used by small aircraft, bringing passengers from Santo Domingo. The newly-built **Arroyo Barril International Airport** in Samaná has yet to meet safety standards.

The domestic airport, **La Isabela**, was built to replace **Herrera** (HEX), 40 minutes north of the centre of Santo Domingo, but it was denied permission to start flights in 2004 because of political problems and large flocks of birds roosting alongside the runway.

Road

Bus   There are two main border posts connecting the Dominican Republic with Haiti. One in the south at Jimaní linking the two capitals, Port-au-Prince and Santo Domingo, and one in the north giving access between the two second cities, Cap Haïtien and Santiago de los Caballeros. By far the easiest way of travelling is with **Terrabús**, which has a service between Pétion-Ville on the outskirts of Port-au-Prince and Santo Domingo, (US$50 one way, US$75 return, US$80 open return). In Santo Domingo the terminal is at Avenida 27 de Febrero esquina Anacaona, Plaza Criolla, **T** 4721080 (departs Sat-Mon 1200, Wed-Fri 0600, 5 hrs). They deal with all border formalities for you, except customs. **Caribe Tours**, **T** 2214422, ext 312, also has a service to and from Haiti, (departs Port-au-Prince daily 0700, departs Santo Domingo daily 1100, US$75 return).

→ Travel extras

Money

The Dominican peso (RD$) is divided into 100 centavos. There are coins of 25c, 50c, 1 peso and 5 pesos, and notes of 5, 10, 20, 50, 100, 500, 1,000 and 2,000 pesos. Away from major centres, it can be difficult to change anything higher than a 500-peso note.

Banks and exchange houses (*casas de cambios*) are authorized to deal in foreign exchange; *cambios* often give better rates. The US dollar is the best currency to bring, but Sterling and Euro can be changed at BanReservas. ATMs are an easy way to get cash and you will get close to the market rate, plus a commission of up to 5%. Travellers' cheques should be in US dollars; you may have difficulty changing them outside of Santo Domingo and tourist places. Nearly all major hotels, restaurants and stores accept most credit cards; inform your bank or credit card company that you are going to the Dominican Republic as there is a high rate of credit card fraud and they may put a stop to your card. The exchange rate is volatile, but in mid-2004 the US dollar was trading at around RD$45 = US$1. See also Directory, p218.

Vaccinations

You should be up to date with your typhoid, tetanus and polio inoculations. The vaccine against infectious hepatitis is a good idea. Malaria prevention is recommended as it is present in the southwest and west of the country. Dengue fever is present in urban areas, and is more prevalent when there has been lots of rain; there is no cure, so protection against mosquitoes is essential. There is rabies, so if you are high risk get yourself vaccinated before you travel. In any case, if you are bitten seek medical help immediately.

Safety

Don't change money on the streets. Be careful with 'helpers' at the airports, who speed your progress through the queues and then charge US$15-20 for their services. Single men have complained of the massive presence of prostitutes. Violent crime against tourists is rare but, as anywhere, watch your money and valuables; avoid walking around Santo Domingo after 2300. Electricity black-outs mean that street lighting is not always efficient. Purse snatchers on motorcycles operate in cities. Keep away from anything to do with illegal drugs; you may be set up and find yourself facing an extended stay in a Dominican prison. Beware of drug-pushers on the Malecón in Santo Domingo and near the Cathedral in Puerto Plata.

If you have anything stolen report the crime at a police station (*politur*, see p223 for details) and get a signed, stamped declaration for your insurance company.

Visas

All visitors (except US and Canadian) require a passport and most need a green tourist card, US$10, purchased from consulates, tourist offices, airlines on departure or at the airport. US and Canadian citizens may enter with a birth certificate or voter registration card and photo ID, but will need a passport to cash TCs, hire a car or make large credit card purchases. Citizens of Argentina, Chile, Ecuador, Iceland, Israel, Japan, Liechtenstein, Peru, South Korea and Uruguay do not need a tourist card to enter. The time limit on tourist cards is 90 days, but if necessary extensions are obtainable from Immigration, Avenida George Washington, Centro de Los Héroes, Santo Domingo, **T** 5348060. The easiest method of extending a tourist card is simply to pay the fine (variable) at the airport when leaving. You should have an outward ticket, although this is not always asked for.

A cheaper, but less comfortable option is the buses run by a syndicate of Dominican operators which leave from rue du Centre between Pavée and des Miracles, Port-au-Prince (Mon-Fri 1100-1200, 7 hrs to Santo Domingo), returning from outside the Haitian embassy, 33 Avenida Juan Sánchez Ramírez, just off Avenida Máximo Gómez between Independencia and Bolívar at around the same time. Your passport must be processed in the embassy before boarding the bus. Take US$25 for border taxes, which have to be paid in dollars cash. Buy Gourdes (Haitian currency) from money changers outside the embassy, or at the border, but no more than US$50-worth, rates are much better in Haiti.

Car Hired cars are not allowed across the border so you cannot rent a car and explore the whole island.

Sea

Many passenger cruise lines call at the Dominican Republic. Santo Domingo and Puerto Plata are the two main cruise ship ports.

Ferries del Caribe has a car and passenger ferry between the Dominican Republic and Puerto Rico, with a capacity for 250 vehicles and 550 passengers. The **Millennium Express**, known as 'El Ferry' (departs Mayagüez Mon, Wed, Fri 2000; departs Santo Domingo Tue, Thu, Sun 2000, 10-12 hrs), costs between US$48-$161 return, for a sleeper cabin for up to four people, including port tax. Contact, in Santo Domingo, **T** 809-6884400, **F** 6884963; in Puerto Rico, **T** 787-8324800, **F** 8311810; or www.ferriesdelcaribe.com. You can arrange onward transport by bus from Mayagüez to San Juan and from Santo Domingo to Terrabús destinations in the Dominican Republic and Haiti.

If arriving on your own boat, the ports of entry are Santo Domingo, La Romana, Luperón, Puerto Plata, Samaná and Punta Cana. You have to clear Customs and Immigration at each port and declare any weapons. Customs fees are US$20 per person and you will be given 30 days' immigration clearance. The port captain and officials have been reported to ask for 'tips' of $20-25 to expedite the paperwork.

Getting around

It is relatively easy to travel around the Dominican Republic. There are several airports with scheduled flights and air taxi services between them. Main roads are in reasonable condition, particularly in the southeast where new highways have been built from the capital out to the beach resorts. Minor roads can be unpredictable and are often unsurfaced. Public transport is varied but good value, and most of the country can be covered using long distance buses, *guaguas* (minibuses or pick-ups); *colectivos* and *carros públicos* (beaten up old cars which run as shared taxis between towns with fixed rates); and *motoconchos* (motorcycle taxis). Car hire is available if you prefer the independence of driving yourself.

Air Santo Domingo (see page 218) has regular flights between Santo Domingo and Puerto Plata (daily, US$56), Punta Cana (daily, US$56), Arroyo Barril, El Portillo and Samaná (Mon-Sat, US$55); there are also flights from Puerto Plata to Punta Cana (daily, US$66). Fly-drive is available from around US$100. Several companies offer air taxi or charter services within the Republic, all based at Herrera Airport; **Caribair** has offices in all national airports (US$185 per plane to Samaná, US$285 to Punta Cana).

Bus

Long distance bus services are efficient and inexpensive, with a wide network and several different companies. The three most comfortable and reliable are **Metro**, **Caribe Tours** and **Terrabús**. **Metro Expreso** (T 5667126) operate from Calle Hatuey esquina Avenida Winston Churchill, near 27 de Febrero. Buses leave daily from Santo Domingo to La Vega (US$3), Santiago (US$4.70), Puerto Plata (US$6), Nagua (US$5), Moca (US$4.50), San Francisco de Macorís (US$4), Sánchez/Samaná (US$5.60) and Castillo (US$4.50). They also have offices in Puerto Plata T 5866063, Santiago T 5839111 and Nagua T 5842259. **Caribe Tours T** 2214422, www.caribetours.com.do, operate from Avenida 27 de Febrero at Leopoldo Navarro. Buses run to all parts of the country except the southeast, including Bonao (US$3), La Vega (US$3.30), Jarabacoa (US$4.70), Santiago (US$4), Barahona (US$4.30), Dajabón/Puerto Plata/Monte Cristi (US$5.70), Sosúa (US$5.30), Sánchez/Samaná/Río San Juan (US$5.30). Most of their services are in air-conditioned buses, with video and toilet. **Terrabús**, Plaza Criolla, Anacaona 15, T 4721080, is an international company with services to Haiti and Puerto Rico (via the ferry, see above), but it also has linked domestic routes to Santiago (T 5873000), Puerto Plata (T 5861977) and Sosúa (T 5711274). Their buses are very comfortable, offering TV, snacks, pillows and blankets, while their terminals have have food shops, toilets, television and children's play area.

Some of the cheaper and less comfortable companies are **Transporte del Cibao**, T 6857210, opposite Parque Enriquillo in Santo Domingo, which goes to Santiago, Dajabón and Puerto Plata; **Transporte Espinal**, four blocks north of Parque Enriquillo, to Santiago, La Vega and Bonao; **La Covacha** buses leave from Parque Enriquillo (Av Duarte and Ravelo) for the east – La Romana, Higüey, Nagua, San Pedro de Macorís, Hato Mayor, Miches; **Astrapu** does the same routes; **Expresos Moto Saad**, Avenida Independencia near Parque Independencia runs 12 daily buses to Bonao, La Vega and Santiago; **Línea Sur** (T 6827682) runs to San Juan, Barahona, Azua and Haiti.

Urban **OMSA** buses run along the main corridors (*corredores*) in Santo Domingo: Avenidas 27 de Febrero, Luperón, Bolívar, Independencia, John F Kennedy, Máximo Gómez and the west of the city, RD$10. *Carros públicos* (shared taxis) have a letter indicating which route they are on and cost RD$10; many congregate at La Rotunda de las Pinas at the intersection of Estrella Sadalhá and Avenida 27 de Febrero. In rural areas it is usually easy to find a *guagua* or *público*. See Taxi section, page 30, for further information.

Car

Dominicans drive on the right. Many of them do not have licences. Local drivers can be erratic so be alert. Hand signals mean only 'I am about to do something.' Watch out for speed bumps at military posts, 'ditches' at road junctions and poorly-lighted vehicles at night. The Autopista Duarte is a good, four-lane highway between Santo Domingo and Santiago, but dangerous. It is used by bicycles and horse-drawn carts as well as motorized vehicles; drivers switch from one lane to the other without warning. The Autovía del Este is an excellent road from Santo Domingo out to the east, with good access roads to Higüey, Punta Cana Airport, Hato Mayor and Sabana de la Mar. The speed limit for city driving is 40 kph, for suburban areas 60 kph and on main roads 80 kph. Service stations generally close at 1800, although some now offer 24-hour service. Gasoline prices rose sharply in 2003, but in dollar terms are around US$2.22 for super unleaded, US$1.50 for diesel. There are tolls on all principal roads out of the capital: RD$15, exact change needed. Road signs are very poor; a detailed map is essential. Expect to be stopped by the police at the entrance to and exit from towns (normally brief and courteous), at junctions in towns, or any speed-restricted area.

If you are hiring a car, a valid driving licence from your country of origin or an international licence is accepted for three months. Avoid the cheapest companies because their vehicles are not usually trustworthy. Prices for small vehicles vary from US$40 to US$90 per day; weekly rates are better value. Credit cards are widely accepted; the cash deposit is normally twice the sum of the contract. The minimum age for hiring a car is usually 25. You can hire motorcycles for US$15 to US$35 a day at most beach resorts. By law, the driver of a motorcycle must wear a crash helmet, but very few do; passengers are not required to wear one. See page 219 for details of hire car companies.

Cycling

You can bring your own bike, but check with your airline if there is a charge and expect a thorough inspection by Customs on arrival. There are bike shops in all major cities and small *repuestos* (repair shops) in almost every town. A helmet is a must; while it is not required by law, the Dominican Republic is not famous for its hospitals. Make sure you get to your destination before sunset as it is extremely dangerous to cycle after dark on or off road. Remember the rules of the road: 'the bigger you are the more right of way you have.' See page 219 for bicycle hire.

Ferry

The only domestic ferry route is from the town of Samaná across the Samaná Bay to Sabana de la Mar. It is run by **Transporte Marítimo Tom Phipps**, T 5382289, (departs Samaná 0900, 1500, returns 1100, 1700). Morning crossings are usually calmer than the afternoon. A pier for a car ferry has been built at Sabana de la Mar but no boat is operating yet.

Taxi

If travelling by private taxi, bargaining is very important and the fare should be negotiated in advance. *Carros públicos*, or *conchos*, are shared taxis normally operating on fixed routes, 24 hours a day, basic fare RD$10, but they can be very crowded. *Públicos* can be hired by one person, if they are empty, and are then called *carreras*. They can be expensive (US$3-4, more on longer routes). Fares are higher at Christmas time. *Públicos/conchos* also run on long-distance routes; ask around to find the cheapest. Motorcycle taxi services, *motoconchos*, RD$15 depending on the length of the journey, sometimes take up to three passengers on pillion. The cost doubles at night. Check your insurance policy as it is unlikely you would be covered for an accident if riding a bike without a helmet. See page 224 for a list of taxi firms.

Tours

Boat tours

Boat trips on catamarans or other sailing yachts can be booked at most beach resorts. At Luperón, on the north coast, a day tour on a catamaran costs US$45, while from Bávaro/Punta Cana it will cost you around US$60. On the Samaná peninsula there are many whale watching tours for about US$40 per person from January to March (see page 77). The boats must be licensed and adhere to strict regulations so as not to interfere with the whales.

City tours

A tour service covers the major sites of Santo Domingo in *merenguaguas parranderas* (buses without seats) **T** 5327154. Recommended travel agents in Santo Domingo for sightseeing tours include: **Metro Tours**, Avenida 27 de Febrero, **T** 5444580; **Domitur**, Avenida N de Cáceres 374, **T** 5307313; **Prieto Tours**, Avenida Francia 125, **T** 6850102; **Coco Tours**, **T** 5861311, www.cocotours.com (city tours on Thu US$49 inc lunch; shopping tours on Sat, US$25) ; and **Turinter**, **T** 6864020, www.turinter.com (city tours US$41, night tours US$39), at Museo del Jamón and Guácara Taína. The **Asociación de Guías de Turismo de la República Dominicana** (Asoguiturd) can be contacted at Calle Vicente C Duarte 3, Apdo Postal 21360, Santo Domingo, **T** 6820209. Nearly all their members speak English and other languages. A two-hour tour of colonial Santo Domingo will cost about US$15, or US$50 for a full day.

Be wary of unofficial English-speaking guides who may approach you. They will refuse to give prices in advance, saying 'pay what you want'. If they are not happy with the tip, they make a scene and threaten to tell the police that you had approached them to deal in drugs.

Cycling tours
See Sports, page 196, for details of cycling and mountain biking tours.

Specialist tours
Sunshine Services, Calle del Carmen 151, Las Terrenas, **T** 2406164, www.sunshineservice.ch, offer tours on the Samaná peninsula and further afield, plus other tourist services. **Espeleogrupo** in Santo Domingo, **T** 6821577, is an educational organization working to protect many anthropological and geological sites, to which they also arrange technical and non-technical excursions, specifically Las Cuevas de Pomier in San Cristóbal and the Cuevas de las Maravillas in La Romana. The **Museo de Historia y Geografía** in Santo Domingo organizes archaeological and historical tours in the Republic; tours are announced in the newspapers, the co-ordinator is Vilma Benzo de Ferrer, **T** 6886952. The **Barahona Ecological Society** welcomes enquiries from Spanish-speaking visitors and offers ecotourism advice, contact Roberto Dominici, **T** 5245081, r.dominici@verizon.net.do. **Julio Féliz** is an English-speaking local guide who specializes in ecotourism and birdwatching, fees negotiable, **T** 5246570, **F** 5243929. **Iguana Mama T** 5710908, www.iguanamama.com, based in Cabarete, offers guided daily mountain biking, hiking and tailor-made cultural and group tours. Also contact them for whitewater rafting, canyoning and cascading, they will put you in touch with the best companies. Iguana Mama donates 10% of its profits to local schools. **Tours Trips Treks & Travel** (4T), also based in Cabarete, **T** 8678884, www.4tdomrep.com, organizes and outfits customized educational adventure expeditions for small or large groups throughout all national parks using national experts and university professors. 4T donates US$1 per client to the DREAM Project, www.dominicandream.org, see page 226 for further details.

Taxi tours

Fares for tours are negotiable, although in busy resort areas such as Punta Cana and Playa Dorada all taxis charge much the same. In places off the beaten track, a *motoconcho* can be hired for a day (US$10-20) or half-day trip, depending on where you want to go.

Walking tours

See Sports, page 200, for details of hiking and tours to national parks.

Tourist information

The head office of the **Secretaría de Estado de Turismo** is in the Edificio de Oficinas Gubernamentales, Avenida México esquina 30 de Marzo, Ala 'D', near the Palacio Nacional, T 2214660, sectur@verizon.net.do, but they do not deal with the general public. There are small tourist offices in most towns. However, private sector operators and guest houses can be a useful source of information.

There are offices at Las Américas International Airport (T 5491496); in Santo Domingo in the colonial city on the first floor of the Palacio Borgella near the Cathedral (T 6863858); Gregorio Luperón Airport at Puerto Plata; in Puerto Plata (Malecón 20, T 5863676); in Santiago (Ayuntamiento, T 5825885); Barahona (T 5243650); Jimaní (T 2483000); Samaná (T 5382332); Boca Chica (T 5235106); San Pedro de Macorís (T 5293644); La Romana (T 5506922); Baní (T 5226018); San Cristóbal (T 5283533); Pedernales (T 5240409); Higüey (T 5542672); El Seíbo (T 5523402); Sosúa (T 5712254); Cabarete (T 5710962); Gaspar Hernández (T 5872485); Río San Juan (T 5892831); Nagua (T 5843862); Las Terrenas (T 2406363); Luperón (T 5718303); Monte Cristi (T 5792254); La Vega (T 2421289); Bonao (T 5253941); and Constanza (T 5392900).

For information about national parks contact the **Secretaría de Estado de Medio Ambiente y Recursos Naturales**,

Subsecretaría de Estado de Areas Protegidas y Biodiversidad, Departamento de Ecoturismo, Avenida Máximo Gómez esquina Reyes Católicos, **T** 4727170 or **T** 4724204 ext 247, www.medioambiente.gov.do, who are very helpful and keen to offer assistance.

Useful websites
www.dominicana.com.do and **www.dominicanrepublic.com** are both Secretaría de Turismo websites; **www.dr1.com** is a private-sector daily news and weather service with a section on travel news; **www.thedominicanrepublic.net** gives listings of businesses with no paid advertising; **www.domrep.ch** for news and information; **www.zonacolonial.com** concentrates on the old city of Santo Domingo with some country-wide information; **www.hispaniola.com** is a good general site; **www.DRpure.com** is great for adventure sports with background information, too. There are a few other local sites, such as **www.samana.com**, **www.samanaonline.com**, **www.cabarete.com**, **www.activecabarete.com**, **www.cabaretekiteboarding.com**, **www.cabaretewindsurfing.com** and **www.puertoplataguide.com**.

Maps
Berndtson & Berndtson publish a good road map, 1:600,000, with detail on Santo Domingo, Puerto Plata and Santiago, available locally for US$5. Scheidig publishes the *Mapa Geográfica de la República Dominicana*, which is approved by the Instituto Geográfico Universitario and available at **Gaar** (Arzobispo Nouel esq Espaillat, Santo Domingo, Mon-Fri 0830-1900, Sat 0930-1500) for US$7. There are several other good maps of the country including Hildebrand, Nelles and Texaco.

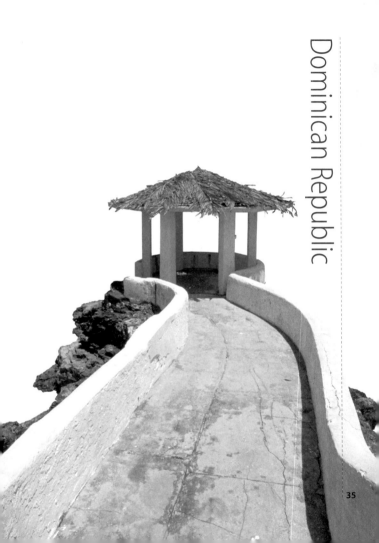

Santo Domingo

Travellers have been marvelling at this city since the beginning of the 16th century, when its streets, fortresses, palaces and churches were the wonder of the Caribbean. Pirates frequently attacked the city, while hurricanes also took their toll on its grand buildings. Restoration of the Zona Colonial, a UNESCO World Cultural Heritage Site, on the west bank of the Río Ozama has made the area very attractive, with open-air cafés and pleasant squares near the waterfront. The colonial city is now only about 1% of the total area of Santo Domingo but it is the first port of call for visitors, holding almost all the sights of historical interest.

Calle Las Damas, which runs alongside the Fortress, is the oldest paved (cobbled) street in the New World and is where the ladies of the court would take their evening promenade. Calle El Conde, a pleasant pedestrian boulevard, runs the length of the colonial city from the entrance gate, Puerta El Conde in the west, to the Fortaleza Ozama and the river in the east.

The rest of Santo Domingo, the first European city in the Western Hemisphere, is busy and modern, sprawling along the Caribbean coast and inland along the banks of the river. Avenida George Washington (also known as the Malecón) runs parallel to the sea; it often becomes an open-air disco, where locals and foreigners dance the merengue. Some of the best museums are west, in the Plaza de la Cultura, while to the east is the monumental lighthouse, Faro a Colón, built to commemorate the 500th anniversary of the arrival of Columbus.

▸▸ *See Sleeping p109, Eating and drinking p140, Bars and clubs p165.*

! In the 1930s, the dictator Rafael Leonidas Trujillo renamed the city Ciudad Trujillo and embarked on a series of public works. After his assassination in 1961 the city immediately reverted to the title of Santo Domingo.

★ Zona Colonial

Catedral Basílica Menor de Santa María

Isabel La Católica esq Nouel. *Mon-Sat 0900-1630, Sun for services. No shorts allowed. Map 1, E5, p252*

This was the first cathedral to be founded in the New World. The first stone was laid by Diego Colón in 1514, it was finished in 1540 and dedicated in 1542. The overall design of the cathedral of Santo Domingo served as a model for others in the Americas: a rectangular ground plan with polygonal apse and a broad central nave twice the width of the aisles and lateral chapels. The nave and side aisles are typical of the 'hall church' mode common in Spain at that time, and the plain round columns support Gothic cross-ribbed vaults. The two main entrances represent the Isabelline and Plateresque phases of architectural design. Little remains of the original interior decoration, because when Sir Francis Drake sacked the city in 1586 his men removed everything of value. The alleged remains of Christopher Columbus were found in 1877 during restoration work. In 1892, the Government of Spain dontated the tomb in which the remains lay until their removal to the Faro a Colón (see page 45). The cathedral was fully restored for 1992, the 500th anniversary of Columbus's first voyage, with new gargoyles, and sculptures at the gates showing the indigenous people when Columbus arrived. A statue to Christopher Columbus (Cristóbal Colón) stands in Parque Colón, with a Taíno woman at his feet, a symbol now considered rather politically incorrect.

Fortaleza Ozama

Calle Las Damas. *Mon-Sat 0900-1900, Sun 1000-1500. US$1. Map 1, F6, p252*

The fortifying of Santo Domingo began in 1503, with the construction of a tower, the Torre de Homenaje, to protect the entrance to the port. From the top you get a great view of the river and the old town and you can see there are two city walls, the outer one built by Trujillo in 1936. The city walls, only partially restored, were started in 1543 by the architect Rodrigo de Liendo. The most important and largest fort, overlooking the river, was the Fortaleza Ozama or Fortaleza de Santo Domingo. It is the oldest fortress in America, constructed 1503-07 by Nicolás de Ovando. There are several remains of buildings around the edge of the fortress, including La Torre, El Polvorín, El Fuerte de Santiago, La Plataforma de Tiro, La Puerta de Carlos III and the new and old walls.

Casa de Don Rodrigo de Bastidas/Museo Infantil

Calle Las Damas, **T** 6855151, www.trampolin.org.do. *Tue-Sun 0800-1700, Sat 0900-1800. US$2, children US$1. Map 1, E6, p252*

A cluster of historical buildings lies either side of Las Damas running north from the Fortaleza Ozama. The first is the Casa de Don Rodrigo de Bastidas, built into the city wall on Calle Las Damas in 1510. This was the house of the royal tax collector and mayor, who went on to colonize Colombia. In 2004 it was remodelled as the Museo Infantil, with rooms encompassing the themes of universe, family, ecology and interactive games. Beside it is the Casa de Ovando, the home of Nicolás de Ovando who contributed greatly to the construction of the city, which has been restored and turned into a splendid hotel, the Sofitel Nicolás de Ovando (see Sleeping, page 109).

Casa de Hernán Cortés

Calle Las Damas. *Map 1, D5, p252*

Dating from the early 16th century, this solid house has been home to numerous government and private occupants, most famously Hernán Cortés, who is said to have planned his trip to conquer Mexico from here. Now it is occupied by the French Embassy and is often referred to as the Casa de Francia.

▶ A city of 'firsts'

The first wooden houses were built in 1496 by Christopher Columbus's (Cristóbal Colón) brother Bartolomé on the eastern bank of the Río Ozama after the failure of settlement on the north coast. In 1498 the Governor, Nicolás de Ovando, moved the city to the other side of the river and started building with stone, a successful move which was continued by Diego Colón, Christopher's son, when he took charge in 1509. For years the city was the base for the Spaniards' exploration and conquest of the continent and it became the first capital city in Spanish America, having the first Audiencia Real, cathedral, university and coinage. In view of this, UNESCO has designated Santo Domingo a World Cultural Heritage Site. However, Santo Domingo's importance waned when Spain set up her colonies in Peru and Mexico with seemingly limitless silver and gold to finance the Crown. Hurricanes managed to sink 15 ships in 1508, 18 in 1509 and many more in later years; in 1562 an earthquake destroyed much of the town. In 1586 Sir Francis Drake attacked from inland where defences were vulnerable, the city was looted, pillaged and set alight. He was the first of many British and French pirates and privateers who attacked in the 16th and 17th centuries. As a result, rebuilding works were continually in progress.

Panteón Nacional

Calle Las Damas entre Mercedes y El Conde. *Tue-Sun 0900-1630. Free. Map 1, D5, p252*

The former Convento de San Ignacio de Loyola, a Jesuit monastery and church, was finished in 1743 but has been the National Pantheon since 1958. It was restored in 1955 by General Trujillo with a generous amount of Italian marble and contains the tombs of, or

★ Best

Places for people watching

- A park bench under the trees in Parque Duarte, Santiago, p61
- Parque Central, Puerto Plata, p65
- Any beach bar in Boca Chica, p81
- Outside tables at Conde de Peñalba restaurant facing Parque Colón, Santo Domingo, p111
- Camilo's restaurant overlooking the Malécon and docks, Samaná, p156

memorials to, many of the country's presidents, heroes and patriots. The remains of General Pedro Santana, five times president, lie here, as do most of his successors. The dictator Trujillo, the 'Benefactor of the Fatherland', intended to rest his bones here, but after his assassination he was not given that honour.

Museo de las Casas Reales
Calle Las Damas, **T** 6824202. *Daily 0900-1700. US$0.60.*
Map 1, D5/6, p252

Constructed in the 16th century, this is one of the most significant historical buildings in the area. In colonial days it was the Palace of the Governors and Captains-General, and of the Audiencia Real and Chancery of the Indies. The Audiencia Real was a supreme court made up of three judges, designed to check the power of the Governor, and its power extended to the rest of the Caribbean and the mainland coast around the Caribbean basin. It is an excellent colonial museum, housing many items salvaged from ships sunk in local waters, as well as furniture, art and military items.

! The *reloj de sol* (sundial) near the end of Las Damas, was built in 1753 so that court officials could tell the time by looking out of their windows.

Plaza España
Calle Las Damas. *Map 1, C5, p252*

Calle Las Damas opens out into the Plaza España, a paved open space surrounded by historical monuments with a statue of Nicolás Ovando in the middle. It has lovely views over the river and many cafés. At night there are often cultural events, such as music, folk dancing or theatre.

Alcázar de Colón
Calle Las Damas y Emilio Tejera. *Mon-Sat 0900-1700, Sun 0900-1600. US$1. Map 1, C6, p252*

A fortified house constructed without any nails by the first Viceroy, Diego Colón, from 1510-14 to house his court and his wife, María de Toledo. It was the seat of the Spanish Crown in the New World and four generations of the Colón family lived here until they left for Spain in 1577 and it was sacked by Drake in 1586. Restoration began in 1957 and it is now a fine example of the architecture of the period, and houses the interesting **Museo Virreinal** (Viceregal Museum).

Museo Naval de la(s) Atarazana(s)
Las Atarazanas, near the Alcázar, **T** 6825834. *Daily 0900-1700. US$0.25. Map 1, B6, p252*

La(s) Atarazana(s), the Dockyards, are a cluster of 16th-century buildings which served as an arsenal, warehouses and taverns for the sailors in port. They have been restored to contain shops, bars and restaurants. The museum contains recovered treasure from several shipwrecks, and exhibits show what life was like on board ship at that time.

Iglesia de Santa Bárbara
Isabel La Católica esq Av Mella. *Map 1, A5, p252*

Santa Bárbara is the patron saint of the military and this is the only joint church and fort in Santo Domingo. Built in 1574 on the site of the city quarry, it was sacked by Drake in 1586, and destroyed by a hurricane in 1591. Reconstructed at the beginning of the 17th century, its design is rather lopsided and haphazard; its two towers are a completely different size and style, and bear little relation to the main entrance with its triple arches. Behind the church are the ruins of its fort.

Museo Mundo de Ambar
Arzobispo Meriño 452, esq Restauración, **T** 6823309. *Mon-Sat 0800-1800, Sun 0000-1300. US$1. Map 1, B4, p252*

Set in a restored 17th-century building, the museum has a fascinating display of scorpions, butterflies and plants fossilized in amber, with microscopes and videos. A guided tour is recommended but not essential. The staff are very informative and will teach you how to tell real amber from fake. Craftsmen polish and shape raw amber for sale.

Monasterio de San Francisco
Hostos esq E Tejera. *Map 1, C4, p252*

Now in ruins, this was the first monastery in the Americas, constructed in the 16th century. Sacked by Drake and destroyed by earthquakes in 1673 and 1751, it has been repeatedly repaired or rebuilt. For about 50 years, until the 1930s, it was used as an asylum for the insane, and there are still metal brackets in places where the patients were restrained with leg chains. Another hurricane closed it down for good and the ruins are now used for cultural events.

"I was so delighted with the scene,
that I had almost come to the resolution
of staying here for the remainder
of my days: for believe me, Sire,
these countries far surpass all the
rest of the world in beauty
and conveniency"

Christopher Columbus writing to the
King and Queen of Spain about the New World

Hospital-Iglesia de San Nicolás de Bari

Hostos entre Mercedes y Luperón. *Map 1, D4, p252*

Completed in 1552, this was the first stone-built hospital in the Americas. The church was used for worship while the two-storey wings were used for wards to cure the sick. Also plundered by Drake, it has survived many earthquakes and hurricanes. In 1911 some of its walls were knocked down because they posed a hazard to passers-by and the last of its valuable wood was taken.

Museo de la Familia Dominicana

Calle Padre Billini esq Arz Meriño, **T** 6895000. *Mon-Sat 0800-1600, US$0.60. Map 1, F4/5, p252*

Housed in the 16th-century Casa de Tostada, home of the writer Francisco de Tostada, the first native professor at the university, who was killed when Drake set about destroying the city in 1586. The museum has a collection of 19th-century furniture, antiques and memorabilia.

● *One block further down Padre Billini is the Convento de los Dominicos, built in 1510. Here in 1538 the first university in the Americas was founded.*

East of the Zona Colonial

Faro a Colón

Parque Mirador del Este, **T** 5911492. *Daily 0900-1700. US$0.60, children, US$0.30. Map 2, C9, p253*

The Faro a Colón (Columbus Lighthouse), built at great cost (and not without controversy) in the Parque Mirador del Este, is in the shape of a cross. Where the arms of the cross intersect is the mausoleum containing the supposed remains of Columbus. When there is sufficient electricity (rare) or a special event, spotlights project a crucifix of light into the night sky, spectacular on a cloudy night. One of the rooms inside the lighthouse is a chapel; others hold exhibitions from different countries.

In the late 1980s, during construction, slums were cleared and some of the 2,000 families evicted received a paltry sum of US$50 before losing their homes. Some 100,000 people are believed to have been adversely affected by the construction work and road building. In light of the controversy, the King and Queen of Spain declined an invitation to attend the 1992 celebrations and the Pope withdrew his acceptance to officially open the building. Two days before the ceremonies were due to begin, President Balaguer's sister inspected the Faro and hours later, she died, inspiring further belief that there was a curse, or *fukú* on the building. Balaguer, who had been held responsible for the whole enterprise, also stayed away from the ceremony while he mourned his sister. The Pope did visit shortly afterwards and said Mass on 11 October. The Pope-mobile is on show outside the building, waiting for the next visit, and his robes are on display inside.

● *Photography inside permitted, but no photos in the museums, no smoking, eating, drinking or pets; guides are free, but tip; shorts above the knee not allowed.*

Tres Ojos

Parque Mirador del Este. *US$1, children and students, US$0.50. Ferry to the furthest lake. Guagua from Parque Enriquillo. Map 3, F8, p253*

East of the Columbus Lighthouse in the Parque Mirador del Este are the *cenotes* (limestone sinkholes) Tres Ojos (Three Eyes), a popular tourist attraction. They used to be public bathing pools in the times of the Taínos, and Anacaona, the wife of Enriquillo, would bathe here. There are concrete walkways, tiled paths and steps down into the caves.

● *At the entrance vendors sell artesanías made from stalactites (light colour) and stalagmites (dark colour), an ecological horror.*

Monumental building

The idea for a lighthouse monument dates back to the mid-19th century, but only in 1927 did it begin to take shape when the Government of the Dominican Republic, with US encouragement, raised a loan to finance a major international architectural competition to find an appropriate design. The Trujillo regime saw it as an opportunity to reclaim for the country the position it had held 400 years earlier, as the hub of transatlantic and intra-American travel and commerce. As a lighthouse, it would be a beacon for ships and planes; as a monument to Columbus, it would emphasize the country's historic and symbolic significance. The winner of the competition, selected from the 10 finalists by a jury that met in Rio de Janeiro in 1931 and included Frank Lloyd Wright, was a young English architect, John Gleave. In his accompanying report Gleave offered a variety of readings for his grandiose design – Aztec serpent, Egyptian sphinx, natural geological formation, modernist abstract architecture – so it could be all things to all people. It was not, however, a functioning lighthouse. The idea of beams of light thrown up from the two arms, although supposedly to guide night-flying aircraft, was more of a metaphor for the way Columbus had brought Christianity to illuminate the Americas. All this accorded perfectly with the ethos of the Trujillo Government, but funding it was to prove difficult.

Construction finally began in 1949, but for most of the next 30 years work was paralyzed and shanty settlements grew up around the building site. In the 1980s, with the quincentennial of Columbus's landfall approaching, work began again in earnest so that another bizarre ruler, the blind Balaguer, could inaugurate the monument he could not see in 1992.

Cuban flag at the Presidential Palace

In 2004, the Cuban flag was hoisted inside the Presidential Palace for the filming of scenes from *The Lost City*, a film by Andy Garcia, starring Robert Duvall and Dustin Hoffman. The script included loud detonations of explosives inside the Palace, as part of the special effects of the film, which recreates Cuba in the late 1950s and the Batista-Castro transition. The local filming of *The Lost City* is part of an effort to boost the Dominican film industry. See Cinema, page 177, for further information.

West of the Zona Colonial

Palacio Presidencial
Doctor Delgado esq Manuel María Castillo, **T** 6958000.
Map 2, D6, p253

Built by Trujillo, the palace is used by the President, but guided tours of the richly decorated interior can be arranged. Opposite the Palacio's grounds, at Avenida México y 30 de Marzo, are the government offices.

Plaza de la Cultura
Av Máximo Gómez, **T** 6873191. *Map 2, D4, p253*

The Plaza de la Cultura, founded by President Balaguer contains the country's major museums alongside the national library and the ultra-modern, white marble National Theatre. All of these museums are under a constant threat of closure due to lack of funds.

▶ José Vela Zanetti

José Vela Zanetti, whose larger-than-life murals and canvases can be seen at the Banco de Reservas and Modern Art Museum (Santo Domingo) and the Monument to the Heroes of the Restoration (Santiago), was an improbable artistic favourite of Trujillo.

Born in Spain in 1912, he fled the country in 1939 after his father was killed by Fascist supporters of Franco. With several other Spanish and Basque artists, he settled in the Dominican Republic, painting prolifically during the 1940s

and 1950s. His most celebrated mural, entitled *The Poor Man's Struggle for Peace*, is to be found in the UN in Manhattan.

Curiously, the Franco-admiring Trujillo commissioned the anarchist painter to decorate his two private mansions around San Cristóbal with murals, although what is left of them is less explicitly social-realist than Zanetti's work elsewhere.

After sojourns in the USA, Mexico and Colombia, Zanetti eventually returned to Spain where he died in 1998.

Museo del Hombre Dominicano

Plaza de la Cultura, **T** 6873622. *Tue-Sun 1000-1700. US$0.60. Map 2, D4, p253*

This museum traces the development of the modern Dominican, from the hunter-gatherer Amerindians in pre-Columbian times, to the Spanish conquerors and the African slaves. The extensive archaeological collection is well displayed, but notices are in Spanish only. Despite the rapid annihilation of the indigenous Taíno population, their influences live on in Dominican life today, in agriculture, fishing, diet, housing, transport, *artesanías* and language. There is also a large display of carnival costumes.

Museo de Arte Moderno

Plaza de la Cultura, **T** 6852154.   *Tue-Sun 1000-1700. US$0.25.*
Map 2, D4, p253

The Museo de Arte Moderno contains a huge amount of
20th-century Dominican art, including works by Jaime Colson,
Candido Bidó and the Spanish exile José Vela Zanetti, see box page
49. Much of the work relates to Taíno themes and *campesino* issues
of poverty and mythology.

Museo de Historia y Geografía

Plaza de la Cultura, **T** 6866668.   *Tue-Sun 1000-1700. US$0.25.*
Map 2, D4, p253

Most of the displays are from the 19th and 20th centuries,
spanning from the Haitian invasion to the American occupation.
A great deal of space is taken up by artefacts belonging to Trujillo,
illustrating his wealth and vanity.
   ● *The museum organizes worthwhile ecological excursions to
different parts of the country, but there is no regular programme and
you have to look in the press for details. The co-ordinator is Vilma
Benzo de Ferrer,* **T** *6886952.*

Jardín Botánico Nacional

Av República de Colombia, Urbanización Los Ríos, **T** 3852611.
Daily 0900-1700. US$0.50, children US$0.40.   Map 2, A1, p253

These botanic gardens have a full classification of the Republic's
flora, and plants endemic to the island are grown here. There are
300 types of orchid, a greenhouse for bromeliads and aquatic
plants, and a beautifully manicured Japanese Garden.

North to Santiago

Santiago de los Caballeros is the busy second city of the Republic in the agricultural heartland. There is an international airport 24 km from Santiago de los Caballeros (see page 22) providing one of the gateways to the north. The Autopista Duarte, a four-lane highway, runs northwest from Santo Domingo with the Cordillera Central on one side and the Cordillera Septentrional on the other. From there it reduces in size, becoming the Carretera Duarte, and follows the length of the Cibao valley alongside the Río Yaque del Norte to its outlet on the coast at Monte Cristi. This is the main artery through the country, used by cars, trucks, *motoconchos*, cows, horse-drawn vehicles and others. The first town of any size just west of the Autopista Duarte is Bonao, 85 km from the centre of Santo Domingo and surrounded by rice paddies. To the east is the Falconbridge ferronickel mine, a large employer and major contributor to the region's economy. The main road to Constanza is off the Autopista Duarte after Bonao. Caribe Tours (Av 27 de Febrero, Las Colinas, **T** 5760790) and Metro Expreso (Maimón y Duarte, **T** 5829111) have daily buses from Santo Domingo and Puerto Plata to the major towns.

▸▸ *See Sleeping p114, Eating and drinking p148, Bars and clubs, p169.*

Heart of the country

Away from the coast, the action-packed heart of the country has some spectacular mountain scenery to offer. The rushing rivers, waterfalls and green forests around Constanza and Jarabacoa provide excellent opportunities for river sports and hiking. The historical city of La Vega is the place to go for Carnival to see the fearsome masks and elaborate costumes.

Sights

Constanza

Direct buses from Santo Domingo, Santiago, La Vega and Bonao. The road from Jarabacoa is passable with an ordinary car in dry weather (1½-2 hrs). The road from the south coast via San José de Ocoa requires a sturdy 4WD. Map 3, D4, p254

High up in the mountains, set in a circular valley formed by a meteor, is Constanza. Dubbed the Alps of the Dominican Republic, the mountains provide a spectacular backdrop for what is a fairly ordinary town. The scenery is some of the best in the country, with rivers, forests and waterfalls and plenty of good hikes. Climbing the Pico de Piñon is a great one-day warm up for Pico Duarte (see page 59). It is rigorous but can be done in about six hours. Some of the trail is sketchy so it is best to take a guide from Rancho Constanza/Cabañas de la Montaña (see page 114), who charge around US$4 per person. In winter, temperatures can fall below 0°C, but during the day it is pleasant and fresh. In the 1950s General Trujillo brought in 200 Japanese families to farm the land, and the valley is famous for the production of potatoes, garlic, strawberries, mushrooms and other vegetables, and for growing ornamental flowers. The main street is Calle Luperón, which runs east to west. Most of the cheap hotels and restaurants are here or nearby. La Isla petrol station is at the east end, where taxis and *motoconchos* congregate. The local tourist office is beside Radio Constanza on Matilde Viñas esquina Abreu, www.constanza.net.

● *A garlic festival is held in June in Constanza.*

Parque Nacional Valle Nuevo

20 km south of Constanza. *Map 3, D5, p254*

With a good, tough, 4WD you can visit the Parque Nacional Valle Nuevo, via the very poor but spectacular road from Constanza to

San José de Ocoa. There are wonderful views and the road passes over the geographical centre of the island, marked by four small pyramids at the Alta Bandera military post, about 30 km south of Constanza. Covering an area of 657 sq km and at an altitude of about 2,640 m, the park's alpine plateau is cold and wet, with temperatures ranging from -5°C and 20°C and an annual average rainfall of over 2,500mm. There are thermal springs, three Amerindian cemeteries and the Aguas Blancas waterfall about 15 km south of town. At weekends or holidays it is very busy and lots of litter accumulates.

The park has a large number of plants, which are unique to the island, in pine and broadleaf forests. Of the 249 plant species found in the park, 97 are endemic. The most common tree is the Creole pine (*Pinus occidentalis*), but, in the west, the huge Dominican magnolia (*Magnolia pallescens*) can be found. It is also good bird watching country. Among the 64 species of birds in the forest, there are two tanagers: the stripe-headed tanager (*Spindalis zena*) and the very pretty blue-hooded euphonia (*Euphonia musica*), which thrives on a diet of mistletoe berries. In the pine trees you can find the pine warbler (*Dendroica pinus*), while in the low trees and thickets lives the white-winged warbler (*Xenoligea montana*), found only on Hispaniola. The ground warbler (*Microligea palustris*) and the rufous-collared sparrow (*Zonotrichia capensis*) also live in the mountains of Hispaniola and go by the local name of *siguita*.

Reserva Científica Ebano Verde

30 km northeast along the road from Constanza. *Map 3, D5, p254*

This cloud forest reserve was created in 1989 to protect the tree of the same name (green ebony). It is managed by the Fundación Progressio, **T** 5651422, **F** 5493900, a private, non-profit organization. The park is very accessible; information is provided on almost every tree, and paths are easy to follow. 621 species of plant have been listed so far, and 59 species of bird, of which 17 are native and 13 endangered, including *el zumbadorcito* (*Mellisuga minima*), the second smallest bird in the world, found only here and in Jamaica.

La Vega

Beside the Highway Duarte, 125km north of Santo Domingo, 40km south of Santiago. *Map 3, C5, p254*

Dating back to 1562, La Vega is a quiet place in the beautiful valley of La Vega Real. In 1805 it was burned to the ground by Haitian invading forces, who spared only the church and a few houses. After the declaration of independence on 27 February 1844, La Vega was the first place to raise the national flag. It was also the first town to embrace the Restoration Movement in 1863. In 1887 a railway was built to Sánchez and the local economy took a leap forward. Several presidents have come from here, including Héctor García Godoy, Juan Bosch and Antonio Guzmán Fernández. The town is nothing special and most people only come here to change buses or to visit the local archaeological sites (see below), which can be reached by hiring a taxi in the Parque Central or at the bus stations.

La Vega's cathedral, **Catedral de la Concepción de la Vega**, on the Parque Central, is a modern, concrete building generally acknowledged as hideous. The **Casa de la Cultura** on Calle Independencia (*Mon-Fri 0930-1200, 1400-1700. Free.*) holds temporary art exhibitions and also has a collection of carnival masks. La Vega's carnival is one of the most colourful pre-Lenten festivities in the country, dating back to 1515. Activities are held on six Sundays in February and March, in the afternoons from 1500-1800. It is estimated that some 1,500 people dress up every Sunday – it is a huge, rowdy affair. See Festivals and Events, page 183, for further details.

Santo Cerro

5 km north of La Vega, the other side of the Autopista Duarte, on the road to Moca. *Map 3, C5, p254*

Santo Cerro is an old convent on top of a hill with a magnificent view over the valley, where the image of Virgen de las Mercedes is venerated and pilgrims come every 24 September to pray. Stories about apparitions of the Virgin and miracles draw crowds of the faithful. Inside the church is a hole in which a cross raised by Christopher Columbus is supposed to have stood. There is also a sign by one of the *níspero* trees by the church saying that it is a descendant of the tree that Columbus used to build the original wooden church. There are several shops selling religious items.

La Vega Vieja

6 km north of La Vega, on the road to Moca, turning on the left by battered sign. *Open most days 0900-1400 depending on numbers of visitors. US$0.50. Map 3, C5, p254*

'Old La Vega' was founded by Columbus in 1494 but destroyed by an earthquake in 1562. Columbus built a fortress, Franciscan monastery and the **Catedral de la Concepción**, which predates Santo Domingo's cathedral and is where the first baptisms of Taínos took place. La Vega Vieja made its money from gold mining and the first mint was started in1502. It was also the first place to grow sugar cane and make sugar.

La Vega Vieja is now a National Historical Park and the foundations of the fortress, church and a few of the 105 houses can still be seen. Most of the ruins are completely overgrown, but there is a small museum, sadly in need of upgrading, which has a fine collection of Taíno tools and ornaments, fossils, pottery, Spanish bowls and tiles, metalwork and armaments.

Museo Hermanas Mirabal

Conuco, 5 km east of Salcedo, just before Tenares on the main road towards San Francisco de Macorís, **T** 5772704. *Daily 0930-1700. US$0.25. Map 3, B6, p254*

The house of the Mirabel sisters is one of the most popular museums in the country. The house was built in 1954 by their mother, Doña Chea, and was the second family home. The gardens are immaculately kept, with beautiful orchids in the trees and lots of other flowers and fruit.

The sisters and their husbands had been active in the resistance movement in the late 1950s, but became martyrs after their deaths in 1960 and are now icons for both liberty and the rights of women. The day of their assassination, 25 November is remembered in many Latin American countries as the International Day Against Violence Towards Women. Their murders helped to lead to the downfall of General Trujillo, who was himself assassinated in May 1961.

The three martyred sisters, Patria, Minerva and María Teresa, lived in this house for the last ten months of their lives, when their husbands were in prison and they were being persecuted by Trujillo's secret police. All three were murdered by Trujillo's henchmen on their way back from visiting their husbands in prison, together with their driver, Rufino de la Cruz, the only man brave enough to take them, given the threat to their lives. The fourth sister, Dedé, did not go with them that day and so survived. She is still alive and in 2000 she opened a library alongside the house, in memory of Dra Minerva Mirabal.

The three sisters are buried in the garden, along with Minerva's hubband, Manolo. They were transferred there from the municipal cemetery in 2000 on the 40th anniversary of the assassination in a ceremony called 'Coming Home' and the mausoleum was declared an extension of the Panteón Nacional (see page 40) where national heroes are interred.

★ Jarabacoa

19 km south of the Autopista Duarte from La Vega.
Map 3, C5, p254

The road to Jarabacoa winds through some beautiful pine forests. The climate is fresh, with warm days and cool nights. It is an important agricultural area, growing coffee, flowers, strawberries, watercress and other crops. The town itself is quite modern: everything is in walking distance and most things can be found along the main street. The vegetable markets in the centre of town are definitely worth a visit. Several notable artists and sculptors live in the area and are willing to receive visitors or give classes.

Mountains, rivers and waterfalls are spectacular features in this area and Jarabacoa is the place to come for adventure sports. The three main rivers are the Río Jimenoa, the Río Baiguate and the Río Yaque del Sur.

Salto Jimenoa

10 km southeast of Jarabacoa, off the road to Constanza.
Daily 0800-1800. US$0.50. Map 3, D5, p254

The Jimenoa waterfalls are large, with a tremendous volume of water and noise, although they are often crowded with tour parties. Hurricane Georges wreaked havoc in 1998, washing away the power plant and bridge by the falls. A new walkway has been made, with wobbly suspension bridges, and a new power station has been built.

Salto Baiguate

4 km northeast of Jarabacoa. *Turn right off the road to La Vega, an easy walk, there is a signpost to the falls, 4th turning on the right after Hotel Pinar Dorado. Map 3, C5, p254*

A concrete path leads from the road around the hillside, hugging the side of the gorge, until you get to some steps down to a sandy river beach and the rocks beneath the falls. It is a beautiful spot and good for river bathing. There are usually lots of tours to the falls by jeep or horse; it's a half-hour ride from Rancho Baiguate.

Parque Nacional José del Carmen Ramírez
Map 3, C3, p254

This national park covers 764 sq km of the southern Cordillera Central and has been a protected area since 1958. The park borders the Parque Nacional Armando Bermúdez (see below) and there is no specific distinction between them. It contains the Yaque del Sur, San Juan and Mijo rivers and the vegetation is classified as subtropical humid mountain forest with conifers and some broadleaf woodland but mostly Creole pine. The Tetero valley also falls within this park, where there are pre-Columbian drawings and rock carvings.

Parque Nacional Armando Bermúdez
Visitors' centre at La Ciénaga de Manabao, see Pico Duarte below. *Map 3, C3, p254*

A protected area since 1956, this 766 sq km park in the northern Cordillera contains the highest peaks in the Caribbean: Pico Duarte (3,087m), La Pelona (3,082m), La Rusilla (3,035m) and Pico Yaque (2,760). This is the largest protected area in the country and provides water for 12 of the country's most important rivers. It is also home to the Hispaniola parrot (*Amazona ventralis*), Hispaniola trogon (*Temnotrogon roseigaster*), the palm chat (*Dulus dominicus*), hutia (*Plagiodonia aedium*) and wild boar (*Sus scropha*). The park contains subtropical humid forest and subtropical rainforest; the highlands are characterized by the endemic Creole pine (*Pinus occidentalis*) and the flora is catalogued according to altitude.

★ Pico Duarte

Ministry of the Environment **T** 4727170 *for latest tariffs and conditions. US$2 national park fees. Guides available at the park entrance, US$5 per day, mules US$3 for baggage, $4 for riding. Guides speak only Spanish; you must pay, feed them and tip them. You are not allowed to set off on your own. Allow US$60 for park entry fee, guide and mule hire for three days.* Guagua *from Jarabacoa to La Ciénaga US$3. On your return the last* carro *for Jarabacoa leaves at 1600. The driest time of year is December to February, but March to November is still good. Map 3, D4/5, p254*

At 3,087 m, Pico Duarte is the highest peak in the Caribbean and climbing it is an unmissable adventure, giving a great sense of achievement when you reach the top. You will see a wide selection of native flora and birds, rainforest and pine forest, and several different ecosystems. If you are not shrouded in cloud, there is a fantastic view looking down on clouds and other mountain peaks.

There are five popular hiking routes requiring different degrees of stamina (La Ciénaga de Manabao; Mata Grande; Constanza; Padre las Casas in the Azua province; and Sabaneta north of San Juan de la Maguana), some taking in other mountains as well. The most popular routes are the 46-km trail from La Ciénaga near Jarabacoa, and the 90-km trail from Mata Grande near San José de las Matas (see below). The Ministry of the Environment enforces limits on departure times from La Ciénaga and Mata Grande. From La Ciénaga to Pico Duarte, Valle de Tetero, and Los Tablones visitors must depart by 1000, 1200, and 1600 respectively. From Mata Grande to Pico Duarte, Loma de Loro and Sabaneta, visitors must depart by 1000, 1600, and 1600 respectively.

From La Ciénaga, allow three days and two nights. There is a Ministry of the Environment centre with campground and visitors' centre with rooms for US$8 a day. Accommodation along the path is in basic huts or the small meteorological station, 1km from the top. The hike is moderate, for intermediate to advanced hikers; mules are definitely recommended for the average hiker, and the guide will want a mule for his gear. Walking sticks/poles are also highly recommended, the journey down can be hard on the knees and dangerous if wet and muddy. Take adequate clothing with you; temperatures can drop below 0°C at night. For a consolidated packing list, visit www.4tdomrep.com/packing.html. Tour operators include Iguana Mama (see page 32) and Tours Trips Treks & Travel in Cabarete (see page 32), and Rancho Baiguate in Jarabacoa (see page 197).

● *During the Trujillo dictatorship, when Pico Duarte was inevitably named Pico Trujillo, one of his geographers erroneously added to the height of the mountain, allegedly to impress his boss. To this day, most maps have Pico Duarte at 3,175m.*

San José de las Matas
38 km southwest of Santiago. *The best road is via Jánico. Map 3, C3, p254*

San José de las Matas is a pleasant, mountain town with tree-lined streets, mostly modern buildings and a breezy climate. The local economy is based on cattle raising, tobacco and food crops. Nearby are the *balnearios* (bathing spots) of Amina, Las Ventanas and Aguas Calientes. There is fishing in the Represa del Río Bao.

Heading south to Mata Grande there is a hiking trail into the Parque Nacional Armando Bermúdez. Take the turning to Mata Grande at Pedregal, from where it is 15 km to the Ministry of the Environment station. The 90-km hike takes five days, three going up via the cloudforest of the Río Bao, La Guácara, Vallecito de los Lilís, up Mount La Pelona, to join the Sabaneta trail, from where you ascend Pico Duarte, and then two days coming down. Guides are required; mules are available at Mata Grande.

Santiago de los Caballeros

Santiago de los Caballeros, 155 km north of Santo Domingo, is the second largest city in the Republic and chief town of the Cibao valley. The streets of the centre are busy and noisy, with lots of advertising signs. East of the centre it becomes greener, cleaner and quieter. The Río Yaque del Norte skirts the city with Avenida Circunvalación running parallel. Santiago is a tourist backwater, there are few sites of tourist interest, although there are some old buildings around Parque Duarte. The Fortaleza San Luís, overlooking the Río Yaque del Norte, is not open to the public as it is a military zone. Calle del Sol is the main commercial street in the old city, with both vendors and the main shops. In the newer part of the town, Avenida Juan Pablo Duarte and Avenida 27 de Febrero have shopping plazas, banks and fast food restaurants, very much in the US style.   Map 3, B4, p254

◉ Sights

Parque Duarte
Bounded on the north by Calle del Sol, on the east by 30 de Marzo, on the south by 16 de Agosto and on the west by Monción.

The Parque Duarte is a pleasant square with a circular bandstand in the middle and large trees under which people sit and pass the time. On the south side is the cream-coloured **Catedral de Santiago Apóstol**, a 19th-century neoclassical building with a green dome, containing the tombs of the tyrant Ulises Heureux and of heroes of the Restauración de la República (see below). Also on the Parque is the **Centro de Recreo**, one of the country's most

In the colonial area look out for tiles on the walls at street corners; they mark the old names of the streets and were put there in 1995 to mark the 500th anniversary of the founding of the city.

exclusive private clubs, and the former Palacio Consistorial (1895-96), now the **Casa de Cultura de Santiago**, which holds art exhibitions (*Calle del Sol, T 2765625, Mon-Sat 0800-1800*).

Monumento a los Héroes de la Restauración
In a park bounded by Av Francia to the west, Las Carreras to the north curving round to join Calle del Sol on the south.

The monument is at the highest point in the city. You can climb up to the top for a panoramic view of the city, the Cibao valley and the mountains. The monument was commissioned by Trujillo in his own honour. A mural by the Spanish artist, Vela Zanetti (see box page 49) was supposed to reflect his glory, but instead he painted peasants and labourers striving for freedom, a point which was apparently lost on Trujillo. Unfortunately, little of the mural remains now. Behind the monument is a theatre built by Balaguer in the 1980s, a rather inpenetrable rectangular block with lots of Italian marble. This area is popular at weekends and fiestas, and there are lots of bars and restaurants around the park. At Carnival or any other outdoor celebration, this is the place to come. Rum shops sprout all over the open spaces, and parades and parties occupy the roads and squares.

León Jiménez tobacco factory
Av 27 de Febrero, **T** 5631111. *Free tour.*

Established in 1903, the factory workers turn out 18 million Marlboro cigarettes a day and 20,000 hand-rolled cigars. No mechanical tools are used, all cigars are completely hand made. The tour is interesting and ends with a free drink and shopping opportunities. There is no obligation to buy, but the shop has a full range of cigars, lighters and cutters.

Know your cigar

Cigar connoisseurs the world over argue about which country produces the best cigars; the Dominican Republic is unquestionably a contender. The area around Santiago is tobacco country. This mountain region has the ideal combination to produce quality tobacco: sunshine, good soil and cool, temperate mountain air.

In the cigar-making process the tobacco leaf comes to the drying room where it is deveined and sorted. The leaves are bunched and cured for anything up to two years. Different leaves are used for different parts of the cigar. There are three parts to a cigar: the filler, the binder and the wrapper. The filler is in the centre and is responsible for determining the strength of the cigar. It comes in three different sections: *volado*, from the base of the plant is light in flavour; *seco* leaves are from the middle; and *ligero*, which has a full-bodied taste, is from the crown of the plant. Binder leaves, used to hold the filler, are from the same plant as the filler and go through the same ageing and curing process. These leaves are either *volado* or *seco*. The wrapper is of the highest quality and ranges from double *claro* (the lightest) to *oscuro* (the darkest). The blending of these three parts determines the overall flavour. For example, the more *volado* and fewer *ligero* leaves the lighter the cigar will be.

Whichever cigars you have, storage is a key element to maintaining their condition. Ideally they should be kept at between 18-19°C and at 70-75% humidity.

The León Jiménez brand is the most widely recognized with a variety of sizes. Another good brand is Flor Dominicana but this is difficult to obtain. When buying cigars it is best to go to the supermarket or corner shop, don't wait until duty free. There are a number of cigar stores in the tourist areas. Be sure to do price comparisons if possible.

Dominican Republic

Centro Cultural Eduardo León Jiménez

Av 27 de Febrero 146, next to the tobacco factory, **T** 5822315, www.centroleon.org.do. *Exhibitions Tue (free), Thu-Sun 0900-1800, Wed 0900-2000. Public areas Tue-Sun 0900-2100. US$1, children under 12 US$0.50. Guided visits US$2 in Spanish, US$2.50 in English, French or German.*

The state-of-the-art cultural centre opened in 2003 in celebration of the 100th anniversary of the founding of the León Jiménez group. There is a visual arts collection, an anthropological collection with some priceless archaeological and ethnological pieces; and a bibliographical collection.

The North Coast

The north coast boasts a stretch of shoreline of immense beauty, with sandy beaches, cliffs, coves and mangroves sandwiched between clear, blue sea and picturesque green mountains. It is home to the historic port of Puerto Plata, fishing villages, all-inclusive resorts and guesthouses. To the west the climate is dry and the vegetation predominantly scrub and cactus, while to the east it is wetter and the vegetation lush, with the ubiquitous coconut palms towering above the beaches and greener-than-green golf courses.

Puerto Plata is the main gateway to the north coast, it has a major international airport (Gregorio Luperón, see page 22), and a busy seaport. The Avenida Circunvalación runs inland, south of the old town, to the airport in the east and Santiago in the west. There are good transport links from Santo Domingo and Santiago with Metro (Beller y 16 de Agosto, **T** 5866062) and Caribe Tours (Caribe Centro Plaza, Camino Real, just off the Circunvalación del Sur, **T** 5864544), and many other bus companies pass through or terminate here.

▸▸ *See Sleeping p117, Eating and drinking p151 and Bars and clubs p170.*

At ease
Yolas at anchor at Cayo Levantado off the Samaná peninsula.

1 *Carnival time in Santo Domingo is an experience not to be missed: colourful costumes, music and parades along the Malecón.* ▶▶ See page 37.

2 *Baseball mania: the game is a national obsession and every young man dreams of stardom. Join the crowds and head to the stadium in San Pedro de Macorís.* ▶▶ See page 82.

3 *An underwater wonderworld: huge tube sponges in a coral garden. There are some excellent dive sites around the country.* ▶▶ See page 197.

4 *Pirates ahoy! Fortaleza San Felipe in Puerto Plata stands firm against invasion from the sea. The poet Pablo Duarte was once held captive here.* ▶▶ See page 65.

5 *Cabarete provides ideal conditions for watersports. Amateurs and professionals alike come here to learn or to take part in the international competitions.* ▶▶ See page 73.

6 *A fearsome carnival mask. The devil is a central character in the pre-lenten festivities.* ▶▶ See page 183.

Whale acrobatics
A humpback male shows off his skills in the waters of Samaná Bay.

North island landscape
Lush, green, rolling hills as far as the eye can see.

Yes, we have no bananas
Plantains of all colours are a staple in the Dominican diet.

Sugar is sweet but the work is hard
Sugar cane is harvested by hand by migrant Haitian workers.

Palapas and palms
Punta Cana has all the elements of the archetypal beach holiday.

Colonial magnificence
The Cathedral in the heart of the old town of Santo Domingo, a UNESCO World Heritage Site.

Puerto Plata and around

Puerto Plata, sandwiched between Mount Isabel de Torres and the sea, is the main gateway on the northern coast, but the town itself is not much visited. The old town centre comprises dilapidated wooden houses and other colonial buildings behind warehouses and the power station alongside the docks. There is some renovation and new building taking place. The seafront drive, the Malecón, sweeps along the beach for about 5 km, between the San Felipe fortress to the west and Long Beach to the east.

Puerto Plata was founded by Nicolás de Ovando in 1502, although Columbus had sailed past the bay and named it the silver port because of the way the sun glistened on the sea. For many years it was used as a supply stop for the silver fleets on their way from Mexico to Spain, but it was prone to pirate attacks and it was eventually supplanted by Havana. It was used by German merchants for trading, and remained an important trading port until the 1960s when investment in tourism and the construction of the Playa Dorada all-inclusive complex just east of the city provided thousands of jobs and became the mainstay of the region's economy. However, it has contributed to the decline of the old city, which has not been able to compete as a tourist attraction. *Map 3, A4, p254*

 Sights

Parque Central
Av Duarte entre José del Carmen Ariza y Separación

The hub of the old town is the Parque Central. In the centre is an early 20th-century bandstand, on the south side is the **San Felipe Cathedral**. Several old houses on the west side of the square are in dire need of renovation and are unused. Also on the Parque Central is the **Patrimonio Cultural** in a majestic building dating from 1908, where there are interesting art exhibitions.

▶ **Amber**

Amber is a golden brown fossilized resin from prehistoric trees, which dripped down the trunk of the tree, before hardening on contact with the air. This glutinous, thick liquid often caught insects, leaves, pollen, seeds, bubbles or drops of water in its path down the tree, preserving them forever.

The first hardened resin is called copal; it takes millions of years to form amber and the oldest pieces found in the Dominican Republic are believed to be 25 million years old. Amber is the only precious or semi-precious stone of vegetable origin and, being vegetable, is much lighter than other precious stones. There are more colours found in Dominican amber than any other; it has tinges of red, green and even blue or black, and is very transparent with lots of well-preserved creatures (a piece of Dominican amber with an intact prehistoric lizard sold for US$130,000 at Christie's in London). Blue amber is very rare and it is found only in the Dominican Republic but it does not contain fossilized insects.

Amber burns easily, being made up of carbon, hydrogen and oxygen $C_{10} H_{16} O$). Amber contains positive electricity and if you rub it against wool it becomes static and small articles like paper will stick to it. Amber fluoresces under ultraviolet light, and this is one of the ways of testing for authenticity. Although the Taínos used amber for personal decoration such as earrings and necklaces, commercial exploitation of the stone for jewellery only really began in the 1950s when Dr Pompilio Brouwer was made Director of Mining by General Trujillo. Trujillo was not interested in amber, he wanted Brouwer to find him gold, not 'those dirty stones', but Brouwer recognized the unique quality of Dominican amber, which was much more plentiful than gold, and began to promote the use of amber in *artesanías*.

Museo del Ambar

Duarte 61 esq Emilio Prud'homme, **T** 5862848,
www.ambermuseum.com. *Mon-Sat 0900-1800. US$1.50.*

The Amber Museum houses a collection of rare and fascinating
pieces of amber from the mines in the Cordillera Septentrional.
These mountains behind Puerto Plata contain the world's richest
deposits of amber and give the area its name of Costa Ambar. An
excellent museum, with well laid-out displays and lots of
information.
● *Amber Museum Shop also at Playa Dorada Plaza, **T** 3202215,
and Marien Coral by Hilton, Costa Dorada, **T** 3201515. Daily
0800-2200.*

Fortaleza de San Felipe
West end of Malecón

Once the era of pirates and privateers had ended, this colonial
fortress, the oldest in the New World (1540), was used as a prison.
Juan Pablo Duarte was locked up here in 1844. The museum is not
especially interesting, but if you climb the turrets you get a
wonderful view of the harbour. Outside there is a statue of General
Luperón on a prancing horse. Nearby, on top of the hill is the
restored **iron lighthouse**, first lit on 9 September 1879, now
surrounded by bits of fortress walls and cannon. It has an
octagonal cast iron cupola supported by columns and used to have
a revolving light and shadow system fuelled by kerosene. It is
24.4m high and the tower has a diameter of 6.2m. It was repaired

! You can swim with dolphins at the Ocean World Adventure
Park from US$50-US$120, www.ocean-world.com. However,
bear in mind that the dophins have been captured against
international treaties, removed from their pods (families) and
fed on a diet of frozen fish and antibiotics.

in 2002 after corrosion by the sea air had put it on the list of the top 100 most endangered buildings by the World Monuments Fund, and is now painted a mustard yellow.

★ Mount Isabel de Torres
Daily except Wed 0830-1700. US$5 round trip. Entrance is south of the Circunvalación del Sur on a paved road marked teleférico. Map 3, A4, p254

One kilometre south of Puerto Plata, a *teleférico* (cable car) runs to the summit of Loma Isabel de Torres, an elevation of 779 m. A statue of Christ looks out from the top over Puerto Plata. There are craft shops, a restaurant and beautifully manicured botanical gardens with a lovely view of the coast and mountains. Morning is the best time to go, as there are fewer clouds and less wind. Hiking alone is not recommended; hiking tours up the mountain can be arranged with Iguana Mama, in Cabarete, see page 32. It is a moderate to hard hike, being quite steep in parts (3 hrs).

Playa Dorada
6 km east of Puerto Plata, 4 km from the airport. *Map 3, A4/5, p254*

The Playa Dorada resort is an umbrella name for the complex of large, all-inclusive hotels with a total of more than 4,000 rooms. The resort has excellent sporting facilities including swimming, tennis and golf, and is best booked as part of a package from abroad. Not all of the hotels are beachfront, but those that aren't have their own beach clubs for guests. There is a central shopping mall, the Playa Dorada Centro Comercial, which has a bank, cinema, tour operators, restaurants and internet access; and plenty of nightlife including discos and casinos. The beach is a glorious sweep of golden sand around the promontory on which most of the hotels stand; the golf course weaves in and out of the hotels not on the beach.

West of Puerto Plata

The northwest coast from Puerto Plata to the Haitian border gradually becomes drier and less hospitable as you go further west. Rice paddies, plantain and tobacco fields give way to scrub, cactus and other plants suited to an arid climate. Mangroves border the river estuaries and grow thickly in the Monte Cristi National Park. The Río Yaque del Norte runs along the fertile Cibao valley, meeting the sea at the Bahía de Monte Cristi. This is the country's most important river and in the 19th century it was used to transport crops and timber to the coast for export. Tourism in the far west is not developed and it is considered as rather a backwater by Dominicans.

 ## Sights

Luperón

Map 3, A3, p254

Luperón, named after General Gregorio Luperón, one of the heroes of the Restauración and president in 1880, is a typical Dominican village, with several markets selling fish, meat and vegetables, basic restaurants and a baseball field. The village jetty is in a lagoon surrounded by mangroves and is a safe harbour for yachts and other boats. Three kilometres from the village is the pretty **Puerto Blanco Marina T** 2994096, *motoconchos* charge less than US$1 from the village, and taxis US$3. This is the place to be with a popular bar, happy hour from 1700-1900 and live music some nights, restaurant, accommodation and catamaran tours.

● *Cat's Sailing Adventure charges US$45 per person for its daily catamaran trips, **T/F** 2612046, catsail@hotmail.com.*

Dominican Republic

Parque Nacional Histórico La Isabela
15 km west of Luperón. *Daily 0800-1745. US$1.20. Take a* público *from Puerto Plata to La Isabela village, then a* motoconcho *to the ruins (US$5 return). Map 3, A3, p254*

Here, on his second voyage, on 29 May 1493, Columbus landed with 1,500 men on 17 ships. He founded the first European town in the Americas, with the first *ayuntamiento* and court and the first mass was said here in 1494 by Fray Bernardo Boil. Only the layout of the town is visible. The restoration and archaeological excavation of La Isabela has uncovered a variety of ruins as well as Taíno and Macorix pottery and the first Hispanic ceramics. The *guayacán* tree (*lignum vitae*) found growing around La Isabela was there before Columbus landed. The wood is very hard and the *guayacán* is used to carve replicas of Taíno artefacts.

Monte Cristi
Far northwestern tip of the Dominican Republic, 270 km from Santo Domingo, 115 km from Santiago. *Map 3, A1, p254*

Monte Cristi is a 19th-century town with a Victorian feel. The surrounding sea is believed to hold the treasures of 179 sunken galleons. A large land and marine park stretches either side of the town along the coast, protecting the mouth of the Río Yaque del Norte. Its proximity to the Haitian border means that transport links are good.

There are several lovely old wooden houses in sore need of renovation. As in Puerto Plata, German merchants started many commercial businesses which included exporting salt, corn, rice, beans and timber, and built comfortable houses with wooden verandas and balconies. The town has an interesting French clock on the Parque Central, or **Parque Reloj**.

During the Trujillo dictatorship, Minerva Mirabal de Tavárez and her husband Manolo had a house on the corner of Santiago

Rodriguez and Henríquez opposite the park. Manolo grew up in the yellow house a couple of houses away, and it was here they they began their revolutionary activities. In the book, *In the Time of the Butterflies*, by Julia Alvarez (see page 237), there is a little diagram of the floor plan of the house.

You can also visit **La Casa de Máximo Gómez** (*Av Mella, opposite Helados Bon, 0900-1200, 1500-1900*), the Dominican patriot who played an important role in the struggle for Cuban independence and in the Dominican Restoration. The small grey house has a plaque above the entrance and contains pictures and mementoes of Máximo Gómez.

The beach at Playa Juan de Bolaños is nothing special and backs onto salt pans, but the coast is dominated by a large flat-topped mountain known as **El Morro**. Steps have been built up the hillside, making an extremely testing climb to a windy viewpoint. On 21 January, the Día de la Virgen Altagracia (see also box, page 90), 2,000 people make a pilgrimage to the top to pray and stay overnight. For further information about festivals and events in Monte Cristi, see page 183.

Cayos Siete Hermanos
1 km offshore in the Parque Nacional Monte Cristi. *Map 3, A1, p254*

The seven cays are a sanctuary for migrating, or seasonal, tropical birds. They have white sand beaches and cacti and are typical tropical desert islands. There has been some destruction of the offshore reefs and there are not as many fish as there used to be because of Haitian fishing incursions, but it is still a worthwhile visit into the national park, where there are several wrecks of old Spanish galleons.

● *Contact the Club Náutico, T 5972530, for fishing or sailing trips, around US$100, or Hervé at Hotel Los Jardines, for snorkelling or diving excursions, around US$50.*

East of Puerto Plata

The coast east of Puerto Plata has some of the most beautiful beaches in the world, set in a green backdrop of mountains descending to a narrow coastal plain, palm trees and sea of all shades of blue. Sosúa, Cabarete and Río San Juan are the main beach destinations, Cabarete being one of the best windsurfing locations in the Caribbean. From all these places you can get quickly up into the mountains for hiking, cycling, horse riding or whatever you fancy away from the beach.

 ## Sights

Sosúa

28 km east of Puerto Plata. *Buses from Santo Domingo US$5.30. Taxi from Puerto Plata US$20,* guagua *US$0.40,* público *US$3.50. Taxi to/from the airport US$14. Transport congregates by the Texaco station and the junction of Calle Dr Rosen and the* carretera. *Map 3, A5, p254*

Sosúa is a little town with a beautiful and lively 1-km beach, perfect for diving and watersports. There is a smaller public beach on the east side of town by Hotel Sosúa by the Sea, referred to as the 'playita', or Little Beach, where you will be less bothered by vendors. The main street is lined with shops, restaurants and bars. The unusual European atmosphere stems from the El Batey side of town (the side that houses most of the hotels and restaurants) which was founded by German-Jewish refugees who settled here in 1941. A synagogue and memorial building are open to the public. The western end of the town is referred to as Los Charamicos (the two ends are separated by the beach); this is the older side of town, where the Dominicans themselves generally live, shop and party.

★ Cabarete

14 km east of Sosúa. *Buses from the coastal road and Puerto Plata. Taxi to the airport US$20, Puerto Plata US$23, Sosúa US$7.* Guagua *to Sosúa US$0.20. Map 3, A6, p254*

Cabarete, famous for world-class windsurfing and kiteboarding, has grown considerably since French-Canadian windsurfers first staked their claim on this small fishing village, but it still maintains its small-town character. There is a wide range of places to stay, eat and dance the night away, with most places along the main road which runs next to the sea. The lagoon behind the main road is good for spotting water birds. The beach is long and sandy with beach bars, romantic dining spots and watersports touting for your business. It is split into two parts, the western end for kiteboarders and the eastern end for windsurfers. International windsurfing competitions are held annually in June, and in February Cabarete hosts an international sandcastle competition. See Festivals and Events, page 182, and Sports, page 202, for further details.

On the outskirts of town is **El Encuentro**, a surfing beach. Close to town is the Parque Nacional El Chocó which has caves believed to be five million years old, and interesting routes for mountain biking and hiking.

Río San Juan

Transport stops at the junction of Duarte and the main road. Caribe Tours T 5892644, to Puerto Plata US$1.70, 1½ hrs, to Samaná US$2.30, 3 hrs. Map 3, A7, p255

At **Laguna Grí Grí**, boats take visitors through the mangrove forests into the lagoon and to see caves and rocks, notably the Cueva de las Golondrinas, formed by an 1846 rockslide. It is several kilometres long and filled with swallows. Tours cost around US$25 per person.

Playa Grande, 5 km east of Río San Juan, is one of the most beautiful beaches on the island. Sadly, it is being developed with large hotels and is packed with people at weekends. This is a good place for surfing in winter and a heaven for golfers (see Sport, page 199). The more secluded and beautiful **Playa La Preciosa**, is the next left turn east after Playa Grande at the headland of the Parque Nacional Cabo Francés Viejo.

Samaná Peninsula

The Samaná peninsula is in the far northeast of the country, geologically the oldest part of the island, a finger of land which used to be separate from the mainland. In the 19th century the bay silted up to such an extent that the two parts joined; the resulting land is now used to grow rice. Previously, the narrow channel between the two was used as a handy escape route by pirates evading larger ships. A ridge of hills runs along the peninsula, green with fields and forests. There are several beautiful beaches, which have not been over-developed or 'improved', fringed with palm trees and interspersed with looming cliffs. The beaches and laid-back lifestyle attracted many Europeans to set up home here, running small hotels and restaurants. Whale watching is a big attraction from January to March, when the humpbacks come to the Bahía de Samaná to breed. This is one of the best places in the world to get close to the whales and a well-organized network of boats takes visitors out to see them.

Sánchez is the gateway town to the peninsula and all road transport passes through here. A good road runs along the southern side of the peninsula to Samaná with a spur over the hills from Sánchez to Las Terrenas on the north side. The El Portillo airport (see page 23) is at Las Terrenas, 8 km from Samaná. If coming from the east of the island you either have to fly, get a bus from Santo Domingo, or take the ferry from Sabana de la Mar (see page 30). There is no road connection through the Parque Nacional Los Haïtises. Buses from the capital are either via San Francisco de Macorís (Caribe Tours, 5 hrs), or via Cotui, Nagua and Sánchez (Caribe Tours and Metro, 4 hrs). Caribe Tours run buses daily from Samaná to Puerto Plata via Sánchez, Nagua, Cabrera, Río San Juan, Gáspar Hernández, Cabarete and Sosúa.

▸▸ *See Sleeping p124, Eating and drinking p156 and Bars and clubs p173.*

Sights

Samaná
Map 3, C10, p255

Santa Bárbara de Samaná, commonly known just as Samaná, is set in a protected harbour, within the Bahía de Samaná. Columbus arrived here on 12 January 1493, but was so fiercely repelled by the Ciguayo Indians that he called the bay the 'Golfo de las Flechas' (the Gulf of Arrows). The town itself is not striking, there are no colonial buildings and no old town to wander around, but the location is very attractive and it is a lively place particularly in whale watching season.

The town was founded in 1756 by families expressly brought from the Canary Islands. The city, reconstructed after being devastated by fire in 1946, shows no evidence of this past, with its modern Catholic church, broad streets, new restaurants and hotels, and noisy motorcycle taxis. In contrast to the Catholic church is a more traditional Protestant church, white with red corrugated-iron roofing, nicknamed locally 'La Churcha'. It came originally from England, donated by the Methodist church, who started the custom of holding harvest festivals which still take place today. The Malecón waterfront road is the main street in the town, lined with restaurants, bars and tour operators. The ferry to Sabana de la Mar leaves from the dock here, as do some whale watching tours and private yacht services.

▶ Humpback whales

A fully grown humpback whale (*Megaptera novaeangliae*) measures 12-15 m and weighs 30-40 tonnes. It is dark grey, or black, with a white belly and long white flippers. On its nose and flippers it has large nodules, not perhaps an attractive feature, but the hairs coming out of the lumps on its nose are used like a cat uses its whiskers. All humpbacks can be identified by the markings on their tails, or flukes, as no two are the same, and scientists have recorded thousands of them so that they can trace and monitor them – they even give them names. Humpbacks are the most agile of whales and perform a variety of acrobatic stunts for the benefit of their rivals or lovers, entertaining human whale watchers in the process. Humpbacks are famous for their singing. Only the males sing and they all sing the same song, repeating phrases over and over again, sometimes for hours, but each year they have a new refrain, a variation on the theme, which they develop during the journey – maybe to keep the kids amused along the way, but more likely to attract a mate.

The humpback is a baleen whale, which means that it scoops up huge gulps of water containing small fish or krill, then sieves it, squeezing the water out between the baleens, retaining the food. When they are in the Bahía de Samaná, Banca Navidad (Navidad Bank) or the Banca de Plata (Silver Bank), they do not feed for the three months of their stay. The water is too warm to support their type of food, although a perfect temperature in which to give birth without harming the calf, which is born without any protective fat to ward off the cold. This fat is soon built up in time for the return journey north to the western north Atlantic and Iceland, by drinking up to 200 litres a day of its mother's milk and putting on weight at a rate of 45 kg a day.

★ Whale watching

Tours available with: Kim Beddall, Whale Samaná, Victoria Marine, Samaná, **T** 5382494, www.whalesamana.com. *Mid-Jan to mid-Mar, 0900 and 1330, US$45;* and with Miguel Bezi, Transporte Marítimo Minadiel, Samaná, **T** 5382556.

Humpback whales return to Samaná Bay at the beginning of every year to mate and calve. The area is recognized as one of the ten best places in the world for whale watching as they are so close to the shore; various companies provide half-day tours, certainly worthwhile if you are in the area at this time. The industry is centred on humpback whales, but pilot whales and spotted dolphins can also be seen in Samaná Bay; bottlenose, spinner and spotted dolphins, Bryde's and other whales can be seen on Silver Bank. The trips to Silver Bank are more educational and are usually arranged by specialist groups. The whole of Samaná Bay, Silver Bank and Navidad Bank is now a National Marine Mammal Sanctuary. During the season the Dirección Nacional de Parques (DNP) monitors the whale watching; they can be contacted at the offices of the Centre for the Conservation and Ecodevelopment of Samaná Bay (CEBSE), **T** 5382042, cebse@verizon.net.do. A set of rules and guidelines has been drawn up by CEBSE, the DNP and the Association of Boat Owners in Samaná to regulate the activities of whale watching boats, including limits on how close they can get to whales and how long they can remain watching them. Data has been collected on the impact on breeding of whale watching, to see if this new tourist attraction has been affecting the humpbacks. There has been no apparent change since 1987 with mothers, calves and singers still in the same area, although more studies are to be undertaken on dive intervals, to see if they are being forced to stay down longer.

● *Often included after a whale watching tour is a trip to Cayo Levantado, known as 'Bacardi Island'. There is a white sand beach, packed at weekends, and good views of the bay. In 2004 the construction of a large new hotel was started.*

Parque Nacional Los Haïtises

*Visits cost US$45 including lunch, with departures from Sánchez, Samaná and Sabana de la Mar. Various companies organize tours (Amilka Tours, **T** 5527664, from Sánchez is the most regular). The Ministry of the Environment in Sabana de la Mar, **T** 5567333, from whom permits must be obtained, offers information.   Map 3, D8, p255*

Across the bay is the Los Haïtises National Park, a fascinating area of 208 sq km of mangroves, humid subtropical forest, seagrass beds, cays, *mogotes* and caves, which were used by the Taínos and later by pirates. The irregular topography of bumpy, green hills was caused by the uplifting of the limestone bedrock and subsequent erosion. There are anthropomorphic cave drawings and other pictures, best seen with a torch, and some carvings. Wooden walkways have been constructed through the caves and into the mangroves in a small area accessible to boats and tourists. The park is rich in birds and wildlife: many of the caves have bats, but there are also manatees and turtles in the mangroves and inland is the endangered solenodon (nez longue). On the Sabana de la Mar side, there is a beautiful two-hour walk through the *mogotes* with a wide variety of vegetation and good bird watching. The humid forest trail is from Caño Hondo to Caño Salado and visits the caves of La Arena, La Línea and San Gabriel.

Las Galeras

From Samaná by guagua US$1.75, by motoconcho US$4.50, 1 hr. Transport congregates where the road ends at the beach. Jeep and motorbike rental on the road to Hotel Moorea Beach. Map 3, C10, p255

At the eastern end of the peninsula, this 1-km beach is framed by the dark rock cliffs and forested mountains of Cape Samaná and Cape Cabrón, now designated a national park. The fishing village is popular with Europeans and Canadians, several of whom have set up small hotels and restaurants. It is a quiet place, unspoilt and delightful; one of the nicest places in the Caribbean to get away from it all. There is very little crime and everyone is friendly and helpful. Most hotels are free of phones and televisions, but there is a communications centre with internet access. There can be weed and coral on the beach, so rubber shoes are a good idea. At the eastern end of the beach is the biggest hotel so far, Casa Marina Bay, an all-inclusive set among masses of coconut palms. The beach here is sandy with no coral and very safe for children.

Playa Rincón

20 mins from Las Galeras by boat. *US$10 return journey, or 40 mins by jeep to Rincón village (8 km), followed by a 2-km rocky and muddy track through coconut palms. Map 3, C10, p255*

Playa Rincón is dominated by the cliffs of 600-m Cape Cabrón and backed by thousands of coconut palms. The sand is soft and there are few corals in the beautifully clear water, but the beach is wild and uncleaned, so coconuts and branches litter the sand. On reaching the beach turn right along a track to get to several beach restaurants at the end where you can get delicious fried fish, caught that morning. They are on a small promontory which gives protection against the waves.

Playa El Valle

10 km dirt road north from Samaná. *4WD needed, or come by boat from Las Terrenas or Las Galeras. A* guagua *(camioneta) comes twice a day from Samaná, US$1. Map 3, C9, p255*

The drive over the mountain is spectacularly beautiful, with two river crossings where women still wash their laundry and children hitch a ride to school. The beach is undeveloped except for a tiny beach bar, aptly named El Paraíso (see page 157). The view from the beach is dramatic, with the headlands rising vertically out of the water and a river running into the sea. Check before swimming at deserted beaches where there can be strong waves and rips; drownings have occurred near El Valle. Ask for advice at the beach bar or at the tiny naval station behind.

Las Terrenas

Taxi from Sánchez (US$20) or motoconcho *(US$3) or from Samaná via El Limón (US$35). Map 3, C9, p255*

On the north coast of the peninsula, Las Terrenas has some of the finest beaches in the country; at low tide you can walk out to coral reefs to see abundant sea life. The beaches go on for miles and are fringed by palm trees. Where the road reaches the shore, at the cemetery in Las Terrenas village, a left turn takes you along a 5-km sandy track past guesthouses and restaurants. At the end of the beach, walk behind a rocky promontory to reach **Playa Bonita**, with hotels, guesthouses and restaurants. Beyond the western tip of this beach is the deserted **Playa Cosón**, a magnificent 6-km arc of white sand (1½ hr walk or US$1 on *motoconcho*). A right turn at the waterfront in Las Terrenas takes you to the largest hotel in the area, El Portillo, behind which is the airstrip.

Salto de Limón

10 km southeast of Las Terrenas on the road to Samaná.
Motoconcho from Las Terrenas to El Limón US$2.50. Map 3, C9, p255

El Limón is a farming village. You can ride or hike for an hour into the hills to a 40-m high waterfall, the Cascada del Limón (or Salto de Limón) which is a national monument and a highly recommended excursion. There are four different access routes to the falls from the Samaná road: Rancho Español, Arroyo Surdido, El Café and El Limón, from which you can hire horses and buy food. If taking a guide, fix the price in advance. Access is regulated to prevent erosion and other damage; visits are only permitted by day on foot or horseback. It is advisable not take valuables to the falls.

The Southeast

The eastern end of the island is generally flatter and drier than the rest, although the hills of the Cordillera Oriental are attractive and provide some great views. Cattle and sugar cane are the predominant agricultural products. However, much of the sugar area has been turned over to more prosperous activities with huge swathes of land put down to golf courses. The main beach resorts are Boca Chica, Juan Dolio, Casa de Campo, Bayahibe, Punta Cana and Bávaro, all with comfortable hotels and watersports. The further east you go, the more remote you become from the rest of the island; excursions from Punta Cana are time consuming.

The *autopista* (toll RD$15) heads east out of Santo Domingo past the international airport towards the beach resorts. Buses run from Santo Domingo along the south coast and stop off at the various turnings to beaches and villages. San Pedro de Macorís is the junction for buses heading north to Hayto Mayor and the ferry at Sabana de la Mar. There are two airports, La Romana International Airport (see page 23) serving the Caso de Campo resort and the hotels at Bayahibe, and Punta Cana International Airport (see page 23), now the busiest in the country.

▸▸ *See Sleeping p129, Eating and drinking p159, Bars and clubs p174.*

Sights

★ Boca Chica

25 km east of Santo Domingo. *Taxi US$15 from airport, US$25 from Santo Domingo. Guagua US$1 from Parque Enriquillo or Parque Independencia, or esq San Martín/Av París, but not after dark; Boca Chica Express bus, US$1, 30-40 mins, until 2100.   Map 3, F9, p255*

The beach town of Boca Chica is the principal resort for the capital. No longer a quiet fishing village, it is packed at weekends with people. There are a couple of large, unexciting hotels and guesthouses and lots of restaurants, bars and nightlife. The main street is closed to traffic at night and the restaurants move their tables onto the streets. The local tourist office is near Coral Hamaca at the end of Calle Duarte, upstairs with *politur*. An increased police presence has reduced levels of crime and prostitution, but the town is yet to shake off its former reputation completely.

Boca Chica is well worth visiting if you want a beach close to Santo Domingo. It is set on a reef-protected shallow lagoon, with a wide sweep of white sand, perfect for families. Offshore a small island, La Matica, offers further protection from currents and a pleasant view across the turquoise water. At weekends vendors on the beach sell local delicacies, which are usually washed down with rum and accompanied by merengue.

Los Guayacanes, **Embassy** and **Juan Dolio** beaches, east of Boca Chica, are popular, especially at weekends when they can be littered and plagued with hawkers (much cleaner and very quiet out of season). The whole area is being developed and a new highway is improving access.

San Pedro de Macorís
On the Río Higuamo. Guaguas *going north leave from near the baseball stadium. Map 3, F10, p255*

This is an industrial sea port whose economy is heavily dependent on sugar. Barceló has its distillery here, producing 75,000 litres of 95° alcohol a day, which is then trucked to Puerto Plata to be turned into rum. There is also an important free trade zone providing low-paid jobs for the town's inhabitants, and the highly respected Universidad Central del Este. It is the third largest city with a population of over 125,000, but it is not really a tourist attraction. It is, however, known for its baseball players; about half of the 500 professional Dominican players in the USA come from here. The local hero is Sammy Sosa, a former shoe-shine boy who beat the world batting record in 1998. As you drive into town from

Juan Dolio you will see the **baseball stadium** with its green roof, known as Play de Beisbol, home of Las Estrellas Orientales.

There is a marked cultural influence from immigrants of the Leeward and Windward Islands, who came in search of labour in the sugar cane fields (now replaced by Haitians). Known as *cocolos*, they perform dances called *guloyas* and *momise*. These take place at the end of June, particularly on 29 June, St Peter's Day, and other festivals. Carnival starts the weekend before Independence Day on 27 February.

Facing the river is the neoclassical cathedral, **San Pablo Apostolo**, with a tower which can be seen all over town. There are many old wooden houses here and around the **Parque Central**, as well as some old warehouses by the docks on the river which desperately need restoring.

Reserva Antropológica de las Cuevas de las Maravillas
Cumayasa, 15 km from San Pedro on the way to La Romana, signed off main road, **T** 6961797, www.cuevadelasmaravillas.com. *Tue-Sun 1000-1800. Adults US$2, children under 12 US$1. Map 3, F10, p255*

This is an excellent new development well worth a detour off the main road when heading east. The huge caves contain stalactites, stalagmites and Taíno drawings, and are now managed by the Ministry of the Environment. There are walkways, steps and ramps through the caves and a knowledgeable guide will accompany you on a 1-hour tour. There is a museum, shop, café, toilets and facilities for wheelchair users. Photography only by prior arrangement.

La Romana
East of San Pedro. *Frequent buses leave from Mercado Modelo behind the church. Map 3, F11, p255*

The town of La Romana is dominated by its sugar factory, which can be seen all along the coast. The town is very spread out, mostly on the west bank of the Río Dulce, which reaches the sea here. Small cruise ships can be accommodated at the mouth of the river, while smaller craft moor beyond the road bridge upriver. Boat trips can be taken both up the river and along the coast. The city has a large Parque Central and, to the north of the square is the church of Santa Rosa de Lima. Otherwise there is not much of interest and most travellers pass through.

Monumento Natural Isla Catalina
Off the coast of La Romana. *Entry US$1. Map 3, F11, p255*

Although inland the southeast part of Isla Catalina (also called Serena Cay) is dry, flat and monotonous, the beaches have fine white sand. The reef provides protected bathing and excellent diving. Cruise ships also call, disgorging some 100,000 passengers in a winter season. The island is under the permanent supervision of the Dominican Navy and the Ministry of the Environment. Tours for US$30-68 including lunch and drinks.

Casa de Campo
10 km east of La Romana. **T** 5233333, www.casadecampo.cc. *Map 3, F11, p255*

This is the premier tourist centre in the Republic. It is kept isolated from the rest of the country behind strict security and is totally self-contained. Covering 7,000 ha, it is vast and exclusive, with miles of luxury villas surrounded by beautifully tended gardens. It has won numerous awards and accolades from travel and specialist sporting magazines.

Sport is the key to the resort's success. There are lots of activities on offer and they are all done professionally and with no expense spared. The tennis club has 13 courts and the riding school has 150 horses for polo, showjumping and trail riding. Above all, however, guests come here for the golf. There are two world-class, 18-hole

★ **Deserted beaches**

• Cayos Siete Hermanos, Monte Cristi, p71
• La Preciosa, Playa Grande, p74
• Playa Rincón, Samaná peninsula, p79
• Playa El Valle, Samaná peninsula, p79
• Bahía Las Aguilas, southwest, p99

courses designed by Pete Dye, one of which is ranked number one in the Caribbean and has seven water holes which challenge even the greatest players.

● *Many famous people have stayed here, including Michael Jackson and Lisa Marie Presley. Bill Clinton is now a regular visitor and Julio Iglesias has a house here.*

★ Altos de Chavón
Free bus every 15 mins from Casa de Campo. Taxi from La Romana US$15-20. Map 3, F11, p255

Altos de Chavón is an international artists' village, built by an Italian cinematographer, in a spectacular hilltop setting above the gorge through which flows the Río Chavón. Students from all over the world come to the art school, but the village is now a major tourist attraction and is linked to Casa de Campo. There are several restaurants, expensive shops and a disco. The **Church of St Stanislaus**, consecrated by Pope John Paul II, contains the ashes of Poland's patron saint and a statue from Krakow. An amphitheatre for open-air concerts seating 5,500 was inaugurated with a show by Frank Sinatra. Many international stars perform here, including Julio Iglesias and Gloria Estefan, as well as the best Dominican performers.

The **Museo Arqueológico Regional** (*Daily 0900-1700. Free.*) is excellent with explanations in Spanish and English and lots of information about how the Taínos lived and their beliefs. There are many representations of bats and owls, which were associated with the souls of the dead, called *opías*, and were the focal point of Taíno religious (*cohoba*) rituals. They were carved in stone or wood with eyes and teeth inlaid with gold or conch. Most of the items date from the 11th to the 15th centuries, although there are some from the 1st to the 10th centuries.

Bayahibe

25 km east of La Romana. Público *from La Romana (US$2.50), or take the Higüey bus to the turning and then a* motoconcho *(US$1). Taxi from La Romana (US$10).* Map 3, F11, p255

Bayahibe is a fishing village on a small bay in a region of dry tropical forest and cactus on the edge of the Parque Nacional del Este, a great place to stay, with excursions, budget lodgings and cafés. Its proximity to the park and the offshore islands has made it the best dive destination in the country (see page 197). A collection of small wooden houses and a church lie on a point between the little bay and a beautiful 1½-km curving white sand beach fringed with palms. There are still lots of rooms and *cabañas* to rent for low-budget travellers, but all-inclusive resorts now dominate the area. Lots of fishing and pleasure boats are moored in the bay and it is from here that boats depart for Isla Saona, part of the Parque Nacional del Este.

Isla Saona

Boat trips US$35-US$50. Map 3, G12, p255

Isla Saona is a picture book tropical island with palm trees and white sandy beaches, set in a protected national park. However it is also an example of mass tourism, which conflicts with its protected status. Every day some 800 tourists are brought on catamarans, speed boats or *lanchas*, for a swim and buffet lunch with rum on the beach. The sea looks like rush hour when the

▶ Archaeological discoveries in the east

The Parque Nacional del Este is gradually revealing its history, as archaeologists explore the inhospitable terrain in search of Taíno relics. The east was heavily populated at the time of Columbus's arrival and it was a politically important area. Cave drawings and carvings have been found, but one of the most important sites so far is the Manantial de la Aleta, reached only by a 24-km, seven-hour difficult mule trail and not open to the public. The Manantial is a *cenote*, a limestone sinkhole 38 m deep; the only way in is through a small opening from where there is a drop of 16 m to the chamber. Many artefacts have been found in the mud at the bottom, dating from 500 years before the conquest, including an elaborately decorated gourd, tools, pots, a wooden serving bowl, food storage vessels and a *duho*, a ceremonial chair used by the *cacique* (chief). It is believed that the *cenote* was used for ceremonial offerings.

When archaeologists were investigating in 1996-97, one of them ran away from a snake and jumped onto a pile of rocks. On closer investigation he discovered it was a wall, which turned out to be the edge of a ball court. Three plazas were found, all about 25 m by 5 m, lined with limestone blocks 1.5 m-2 m high, indicating that this was a major settlement, possibly the village of the *cacique* Cotubanamá, where a massacre took place in 1503. While Indian slaves were loading bread onto a Spanish ship, a Spaniard released his dog, which attacked a *cacique* and disembowelled him. Three Spaniards were later killed in revenge and this unleashed the full wrath of the colonizing power, ending in slaughter on a huge scale. Bartolomé de las Casas, the Spanish historian who did so much to bring the atrocities against the Indians to public attention, reported seeing 700 bodies laid out in a plaza.

boats come and go. If you arrange a trip independently on a *lancha*, a smaller, slower boat, the local association of boat owners assures uniform prices.

Parque Nacional del Este
Map 3, F12, p255

The Parque Nacional del Este (430 sq km) is on the peninsula south of San Rafael de Yuma between the villages of Bayahibe and Boca de Yuma and includes the islands of Saona, Catalina and Catalinita. It is a combination of subtropical humid forest and dry forest, with a large number of endemic trees. It has remote beaches and is the habitat of the now scarce crowned or white-headed dove (*Columba leucocephala*), the rhinoceros iguana and various turtles. 112 species of bird have been registered here, of which eight are endemic to the island and 11 endemic to the Caribbean. The solenodon and the hutia have been sighted and marine mammals include the manatee and the bottlenose dolphin.

The geology of the area includes a number of caves, many of which are believed to be linked in an underground tunnel system. Some of the caves contain pre-Columbian pictographs (drawings) and petroglyphs (carvings). Uncontrolled visits to the caves by tourists have caused damage to their internal microclimates and disturbed the bats. Visitors must pay a fee at the Ministry of the Environment office and hire a guide.

Motorboats to the beach areas affect the manatees, dolphins, turtles and iguanas, while fuel and lubricants accumulate on the beach and pollute the water. Encroachment by hotels at the edge of the park is whittling away at the size of the protected area and in 2004 there was an international campaign to prevent a Spanish company building yet another resort following a legally dubious land purchase.

Higüey
Map 3, E12, p255

The main town in the far east of the island is the modern, dusty and concrete Higüey. The focal point of interest is the **Basílica de Nuestra Señora de la Altagracia** (patroness of the Republic), an impressive modern building to which every year there is a pilgrimage on 21 January. According to legend, the Virgin appeared in 1691 in an orange tree to a sick girl; oranges are conveniently in season in January and huge piles of them are sold on the streets. The Basílica was started by Trujillo in 1954, but finished by Balaguer in 1972. The theme throughout is of the orange tree, with wood of the orange tree used extensively. People wearing shorts are not allowed to enter. The old 17th-century church, which used to be the site of the pilgrimage, was restored at the beginning of the 20th century after earthquake damage.

Casa de Ponce de León
San Rafael de Yuma, south of Higüey, east of Bayahibe. *Turn left in the town, take the unpaved road past the primary school and drive for 1 km to the entrance, which is on the right by an electricity pole. There is no sign.* *Map 3, F12, p255*

Juan Ponce de León was in charge of the military campaign which conquered the Higüey *cacicazgo* in 1507 and he was made lieutenant governor of Higüey by Governor Nicolás de Ovando. He took over the Indians' agricultural holdings and maintained a prosperous hacienda which helped to finance his later explorations of the Americas. The Casa de Ponce de León is an important historical landmark, one of the oldest fortified houses (casa fortaleza), built 1505-08 by Indian slaves. It is known locally as Las Ruinas, but in fact it has been restored and is in excellent condition, containing items supposedly belonging to Ponce de León.

▶ La Virgen de la Altagracia
20-21 January, Higüey

Higüey, the night before the day the Virgin was supposed to have appeared in an orange tree to a sick girl. The town celebrates this important religious event with a mixture of the religious and the profane. A queue of pilgrims from all over the country, and even from abroad, snakes around the park around the Basílica, lit by the flicker of candles as they wait their turn to touch the glass covering the picture of La Virgen de la Altagracia. Tomorrow she will be taken around the town in a slow procession accompanied by a brass band.

Outside the Basílica walls, the town is a huge market and fairground where all manner of items are for sale, from trainers to blow up Father Christmases, while everywhere there are huge piles of oranges on display. A park has been converted into a fairground with a big wheel, a merry-go-round and lots of games of chance, but taking up most of the space are hundreds of rum shops doing excellent business. Live bands play and a massive sound system drowns out any conversation, but who cares when the rum is flowing?

Pilgrims have walked or found some alternative means of transport to get here and the hotels are full to over- flowing. If anyone sleeps it will be a miracle, unless the rum anaesthetizes them. Several bodies can be seen lying under parked cars or curled up in doorways.

Apart from the occasional respite, the music blares forth all through the night, accompanied by fireworks, *motoconchos*, car alarms and raised voices. In the early hours of the morning, the Basílica starts to broadcast a continuous religious service over a loud-speaker to the whole town, competing with the merengue for people's attention.

Punta Cana/Bávaro

On the coast due east from Higüey, 3 hrs by road from Santo Domingo. *Map 3, E13, p255*

Punta Cana and Bávaro attract thousands of tourists each year because of their stunning pure white beaches, fringed with coconut palms, and calm blue seas with crystal-clear water. The area away from the beach is not particularly pretty – the land is flat and the vegetation is mostly scrub and cactus. The area was virtually untouched until Club Med opened in 1981, followed by the Punta Cana Beach Resort in 1988, a golf course runs between them. The Marina Punta Cana has a capacity for 22 yachts (24-hrs' notice required if arriving by sea).

On the northern side of the 'toe' of the island, is the area now known as **Bávaro**, where there are many other white sand beaches, coconut palms and reef-sheltered water. Bávaro was once a series of fishing villages, but they have disappeared under the encroachment of the hotels. Hotels are usually booked from abroad as package holidays and most of them are all-inclusive, run by international companies.

Playa el Cortecito is a little oasis, a breath of fresh air in amongst the all-inclusives, and is the nearest thing to a village that you will find on this stretch of coast. There are several beach bars, restaurants, gift shops, a supermarket, watersports, internet access and tour operators. It is a lively place and makes a welcome change from the all-inclusive lifestyle.

Bibijagua is just along the beach from the Barceló complex. The Mercado Artesanal is a large covered market on the beach where you can buy handicrafts and souvenirs. Don't buy the shells, turtles and stuffed sharks as they are protected by international treaties and will be impounded by customs officials on your return home.

The Southwest

The far southwest of the Republic is a mostly dry zone with typical dry-forest vegetation, but offers a range of climatic zones including low-mountain rainforest. It also contains some of the country's most spectacular coastline and several national parks. It is a mountainous area with great views and twisting roads, and the closer you get to the Haitian border the poorer and more deforested the country becomes. This was the major cause of the devastation after heavy rains in 2004. It may never be known how many thousands of people lost their lives in mud slides at Jimaní and across the border in Haiti, where there were no trees to hold the soil in place. Tourism is not big business here yet, although there are some fascinating places to visit, such as Lago Enriquillo, a saltwater lake below sea level and three times saltier than the sea, or the mines for larimar, a pale blue semi-precious stone used in jewellery. The towns are unremarkable, but give a fascinating insight into rural and provincial life in the Republic.

▸▸ *See Sleeping p134 and Eating and drinking p160.*

Towards Barahona

Heading west from Santo Domingo, there is a good toll highway (RD$15) passing through San Cristóbal to the sugar-producing town of Baní. The main road continues northwest to the port of Azua de Compostela before heading inland and rejoining the coast at Barahona. There is the María Montéz International Airport at Barahona, but it is rarely used. Most people arrive by road and there are good long-distance bus connections with Santo Domingo to the major towns.

Sights

San Cristóbal

25 km west of Santo Domingo *Map 3, F7, p255*

The birthplace of the dictator Trujillo, most sites of interest are related to his involvement with the town, where he had two houses. During his long period in power Trujillo changed the town's name to 'Meritorious City'. He lavished large sums of money on public and private buildings, but to little aesthetic effect. The **Iglesia Parroquial**, an imposing mustard-yellow church, was reputedly built at great expense in the 1940s as the last planned resting place of Trujillo (until he thought of El Panteón in Santo Domingo). Inside is a large mural by the Spanish artist, José Vela Zanetti (see box, page 49). Other attractions in town include the grand **Palacio del Ayuntamiento**, on the corner of Avenida Constitución and Calle Padre Brown, in which the Republic's first constitution was signed in 1844. A plaque commemorates the event. A busy industrial and commercial centre, San Cristóbal does not have great charm, you can bypass it by taking the toll road.

Both of Trujillo's homes are now in ruins but can be visited. The **Casa de Caoba** was looted and stripped bare after the dictator's death, but still gives an idea of the building's former opulence, when it was lined with mahogany. Take the turning off the dual carriageway from Santo Domingo signed to La Toma de San Cristóbal, bypassing the city. Turn right after the purple PLD office and then stop just after the water tank on your left. The 1-km road up to the house is on your left, but a sturdy 4WD is required – it is better to walk. A caretaker will let you in and show you around for a tip.

The **Palacio del Cerro** was another luxury residence on top of a hill with a tremendous view. The Palacio is run down, although there are more decorative features than at the Casa de Caoba, including a grand marble staircase, a gold and silver mosaic-tiled bathroom, the salón de fiestas with its pink and chocolate-brown ceiling, and a heliport on the roof. From the Parque Central follow the Baní road, Avenida Luperón, and turn left at the Isla petrol station. The house is guarded by the military, but for a tip someone will show you around.

El Pomier Caves

15 km north of San Cristóbal on the road to La Toma de San Cristóbal. *Buses from Parque Central, Mon-Sat 1000-1600. US$2 for tour. Map 3, F7, p255*

The **Reserva Antropológica de las Cuevas de Borbón** was extended in 1996 to protect the El Pomier caves, under threat from limestone quarrying. Eight new fauna species have since been found here and more are suspected to inhabit the less accessible caverns. The caves are of enormous archeological value, considered to be as important for the Caribbean Basin as Egypt's pyramids are for the Middle East. The reserve comprises over 6,000 paintings and some 500 rupestrian engravings. Cave One has been fitted with special lights and ramps, giving access to all. Tours Trips Treks & Travel (see page 32) offers customized educational adventures for groups into many of the caves closed to the public. On the local saint's day festival (6-10 June) religious ceremonies take place around the caves.

● *Nearby are **La Toma** natural pools, for swimming, open Mon-Fri 0900-1800, Sat-Sun 0700-1930, US$1. They serve as a significant source of drinking water for the city of San Cristóbal.*

Las Salinas

Map 3, G5, p254

To get to the fishing village of Las Salinas from San Cristóbal, follow the main road to **Baní**. Of the two roads west out of Baní, take the one to Las Calderas naval base; there is no problem with going through the base, but photography is not allowed. After the base, turn left and it is 3 km to the village. The road passes the unique sand dunes of the **Bahía de Calderas**, now a national monument, and an inlet on the **Bahía de Ocoa**, shallow, with some mangroves and good windsurfing and fishing. The dunes, which can be reached from the road, have spectacular views, but there are no facilities and little shade. At the end of the road is the Parador Turístico Punta Salinas, a public beach with restaurant, disco and *politur* station. Completely deserted during the week, it springs into life at weekends and holidays when people come to eat, drink and party. The beach is grey sand, but it is kept reasonably clean.

Barahona

By road from Santo Domingo, 3 hrs. Minibus US$3, público *US$4, Caribe Tours runs 4 buses a day. From Jimaní 2½ hrs, US$3.30. Map 3, G3, p254*

Barahona is a comparatively young town, founded in 1802 by the Haitian leader, Toussaint Louverture, when he was briefly in control of the whole of Hispaniola. Its economy initially rested on the export to Europe of precious woods, but in the 20th century the sugar industry took over. The main attractions of this rather rundown grid-system town revolve around the seafront Malecón, where most hotels and restaurants are to be found. The Parque Central, five blocks up, is the commercial hub and a pleasant spot, although tourists are liable to be pestered. The small, public beach at Barahona is filthy and theft is common. Eco Tour (see page 226) and Tours Trips Treks & Travel (see page 32) offer customized educational adventure tours to the national parks nearby.

The far southwest

Those with a car can visit the remote beaches south of Barahona (public transport is limited to públicos). The coast road south of Barahona runs through some of the most beautiful scenery in the Republic, with mountains on one side, the sea on the other, leading to the Haitian border (146 km). All along the southern coast are many white sand beaches with some of the best snorkelling in the Republic. The road north from Pedernales to Jimaní is very rough, and impassable without a 4WD, but runs through lush and mountainous countryside along the Haitian border and cuts through the Parque Nacional Sierra de Bahoruco.

Sights

Larimar mines

Just before Baoruco, at the end of Las Filipinas, 14 km south of Barahona, turn right onto a dirt road for 15 km into the hills along a very poor track to Los Chupaderos, the mine is at the end of the road (4WD essential, especially after rain, ask for directions at the nearby colmado). Map 3, G3, p254

High up in the lush forested mountains are the open-cast mines where the semi-precious mineral, larimar, is dug from a labyrinth of tunnels. Larimar is mined only in the Dominican Republic and is mostly used for jewellery. It is a pale blue or turquoise hard stone flecked with cream or white. The primitive mines are worth a visit, and it is a beautiful drive with views down to the coast, but they will be closed if it rains as the mines flood. Miners or local boys will sell you fragments of stone by weight, usually in jars of water to enhance the colour, for US$5-10. When dry, larimar is a paler blue.

South of Barahona
Map 3, G3-H2, p254

The first place you reach is the pebble beach of **El Quemaito**, where the river comes out of the beach, the cold fresh water mixing with the warm sea; offshore is a reef. Back on the main road, you pass through **Baoruco** (see Sleeping page 135) and **La Ciénaga** which have small stony beaches and rough tides. The road comes right down to the sea before **San Rafael** natural springs (about 40 mins from Barahona) where the forest grows to the edge of the stony beach and a river runs out. There is a *pensión* where the road crosses the river, with a free cold-water swimming hole behind it (safer than the sea as enormous waves surge onto the beach); at weekends it gets very crowded. It is also possible to climb up the mountain alongside the river, which has small waterfalls and pools. Most of these beaches have domestic animals, so there are droppings on the sand. The coastal road hugs the Caribbean Sea leading through the medium-sized town of **El Paraíso**, 31 km from Barahona, which has a popular beach and many *colmados*, *cafeterías* and bars.

At **Los Patos** another river flows into the sea to form a cool bathing place, with excellent swimming and lots of family groups. Restaurante Los Patos has a small pool and good seafood. La Chorrea is a man-made pool from a natural spring about five minutes' drive up a dirt road on the right-hand side. There are cool, freshwater lagoons behind several of the other beaches on this stretch of coast. Laguna Limón is a flamingo reserve. Roads are dangerous at night and impassable without 4WD after rain.

West to Pedernales
Map 3, H2-G1, p254

Enriquillo, 54 km south of Barahona, is the last place for fuel until Pedernales, 80 km away, but no unleaded is available. After

Enriquillo the road turns inland up to **Oviedo** and then skirts the Parque Nacional Jaragua. Oviedo, with the atmosphere of a desert settlement, has a telephone centre but no hotels or decent restaurants, and is one of the hottest places in the country. About 5 km after Oviedo, **Manuel Goya** has the last café before the border. **Pozo Trinicolas** is a chance for a refreshing break and a cool dip in the middle of the desert of the Jaragua National Park. Just after a double S-curve, look for a small parking area on the left-hand side about 14 km before Pedernales. Three clear pools fed by subterranean rivers flowing from the Sierra de Neiba surface here. If there has been recent rainfall, bring your mosquito repellent.

Parque Nacional Jaragua
Ministry of the Environment office just outside Oviedo in Cajuil. *Daily 0830-1630, US$1. Boat tour of the lagoon for up to 8 visitors US$35. Map 3, H1, p254*

Parque Nacional Jaragua is the largest of the Dominican Republic's national parks at over 900 sq km. This area of subtropical dry forest and inhospitable prickly scrub also contains a marine zone, in which lie the uninhabited islands of **Beata** and **Alto Velo**. The vegetation is largely cactus and other desert plants, but there are also mahogany, frangipani and extensive mangroves. Of particular interest is the **Laguna Oviedo** at the eastern end of the park, which is accessible from Oviedo and Barahona. The lagoon contains the country's largest population of flamingos as well as herons, terns, spoonbills and frigate birds. Animals include the ricord iguana, the rhinoceros iguana, 11 species of bat, and four species of marine turtle which climb up the park's beaches to lay their eggs.

Turn left onto a rough track after the DNP office to reach a hut where the park official, Señor Blanco, is a knowledgeable guide (Spanish speaking); he will point out birds and iguanas and take visitors to Taíno cave sites. He is also responsible for initiating the conservation efforts to protect unhatched turtle eggs. Archaeological finds point to indigenous settlement dating from 2590BC and there are pictographs and petrographs in caves at Guannal, La Cueva La Poza and Cueva Mongó.

Bahía de las Aguilas
Map 3, H1, p254

Bahía de las Aguilas is one of the most pristine and virginal beaches in the country, although government and big business frequently threaten to develop the area. From Oviedo, continue on Route 44 towards Pedernales. At the intersection of Cabo Rojo, head south towards the Ideal Dominicana, and then on an unpaved road along the coast heading east to the small fishing community called La Cueva. Resourceful members of the community have converted the caves into homes. A small Ministry of the Environment shack collects the fee (US$1). Primitive camping areas abound, and there is even a small cabin located toward the western end of the bay above the dunes. From here boats cost around US$25 for the 30-minute journey to the white sandy beach and desolate shores. A dangerous 6-km 4WD road also runs to the beach. Make sure you bring anything you need, including food and water, as there are absolutely no services available in the area. Remember to pay your boat driver only after he has picked you up for the return journey.

Pedernales
Map 3, G1, p254

Pedernales is the most westerly town of the Republic, on the Haitian border. This is a major crossing point for migrant Haitian workers who come over to work in the sugar cane plantations and in construction.

There is no immigration office so in theory only Haitians may enter Haiti here. However, border guards are willing to turn a blind eye in return for a small sum (US$10 or so). It is advised that you make yourself known at the Anse-à-Pitres police station on the Haitian side and that you return within a few hours. If there is a change of personnel at the border station, you may find yourself paying another 'tip'. There is no road link, but the crossing can be done on foot if the stream that divides the countries is not too high, or you can hire a *motoconcho*. Every Friday there is an informal market in the no man's land at the border crossing, where Haitians sell cheap counterfeit clothing brands, smuggled spirits and a vast array of plastic kitchenware.

Parque Nacional Sierra de Bahoruco

From route 44 at the Cabo Rojo intersection head north (away from Bahía de las Aguilas) for about 1 hr to reach Hoyo de Pelompito. US$1. Map 3, G1, p254

The Sierra de Bahoruco National Park covers 800 sq km of land ranging from sea level to 2,367 m. It is a very mountainous area, of mainly crystallized limestone, and is believed to have been formed about 50 million years ago. The vegetation varies from dry forest at sea level to mountain humid and rain forest, with large areas of pine, broad-leaf forest and mixed forest. The park has 1,268 plant species, including 55% of the orchid species found in the Republic, 32 of which are endemic to the sierra. It also has 49 species of bird, of which 19 are endemic, including the stolid flycatcher (*Myiarchus stolidus*), Hispaniola lizard cuckoo (*Saurothera longirostris*), and the white-necked crow (*Corvus leucognaphalus*). The **Hoyo de Pelompito** is an interesting mountain depression offering beautiful vistas of the park, informative panels, bathrooms, and picnic area.

Valle de Neiba

The Neiba valley lies between Barahona and the border town of Jimaní. Much of the area has been dedicated to national parks and is dominated by the excessively saline Lago Enriquillo in the west and the freshwater Laguna Ovieda in the east. If you have your own transport, the road north of the lake is the most interesting route from Neiba to Jimaní. There are daily buses to Jimaní from Santo Domingo using the southern route (see page 23).

 Sights

Parque Nacional de Cabral
30 km west of Barahona. *Map 3, F3, p254*

The **Laguna Rincón** or de Cabral National Park covers over 240 sq km in the Neiba valley. It is the second largest lagoon and the largest freshwater lagoon in the country. Water lilies and other freshwater plants provide a habitat for freshwater shrimp and some endemic fish, but notably there is a large population of the Hispaniolan freshwater slider turtle (*Trachemys decorata*), which is also endemic. Several ducks can be found on the lagoon, including the masked duck and the ruddy duck, as well as heron, ibis, teal and flamingo. Thousands of migratory birds from North America touch down here, and many kinds of shallow-water wading birds make the lagoon their home. Reptiles like the rhinoceros iguana, lizards, snakes, giant toads and the Dominican tree frog (*Osteopilus dominicensis*) also live here.

● *At Cabral there is a turning marked 'Polo'. This will take you to a place known as 'Polo Magnético', a spot where the road appears to rise. If you roll a ball along the road it looks as though it is rolling uphill, a strange optical illusion.*

Las Caritas
Map 3, E1, p256

The road along the north shore of Lago Enriquillo, west of Neiba, gives you glimpses of the lake as you pass through the villages. After Río Postrer you come close to the lake. Look for a sign on your right for Las Caritas and stop at the side of the road. You can clamber up the rocks to an arch, or cave, on the hillside where there are pictographs. Faces (*caritas*) have been drawn on the coral rock by the Taínos. From the shade of the arch you can get a lovely view over the lake and watch the flamingos wading at the shoreline. From here it is a few minutes to La Azufrada and the sign for Lago Enriquillo.

★ Parque Nacional Isla Cabritos
Ministry of the Environment ranger station east of La Descubierta at La Azufrada. *0700-1500. US$1 Map 3, F1, p256*

The 200-sq-km **Lago Enriquillo**, whose waters are three times saltier than the sea, was cut off from the sea by tectonic movements several million years ago. The surrounding beaches and the islands are rich in ancient seashells and coral fragments. At La Azufrada there is a sulphur pool, beautifully clean and clear, but not particularly warm. Three islands in the lake, Isla Cabritos, Barbarita and La Islita, together with the lake and surrounding shoreline, make up the Parque Nacional Isla Cabritos. It is a unique environment, 4-40 m below sea level and there is no fresh water on the islands. The park has numerous species of reptile including the endangered rhinoceros and ricord iguanas and one of the largest wild American crocodile populations in the world.

Only groups with a guide are permitted to go to Isla Cabritos. There is usually a boat waiting to take parties over, US$15 for the 30-minute trip, which leaves when full. There is a café, but take water on the boat. On arrival at Isla Cabritos, there is a museum and information centre. There are also three walking trails from where you can see the crocodiles.

The last of the caciques

Honoured by a statue near Cabral, and by a lake and a town named after him, the legendary Enriquillo looms large in Dominican history and mythology. While other caciques or Taíno chieftains rapidly succumbed to the violence and disease spread by the early Spanish colonists, Enriquillo fought back, and his resistance has become part of the country's popular traditions.

Orphaned at an early age, he was educated by Franciscan friars in Santo Domingo before being sent to lead an *encomienda*, a community of Taínos forced to work for a Spanish landowner. Conscious of the iniquities of the *encomienda* system, Enriquillo argued with his Spanish master and appealed to the Real Audiencia, without success. He escaped with a number of followers into the impenetrable mountains of the Sierra de Bahoruco, forming an independent state which refused to recognize Spanish ownership of the island. Enriquillo led a national war of liberation from 1519-1533, launching guerrilla attacks on Spanish settlements. He later signed a peace treaty, before his death in 1535. His 2,000 followers were given a small reservation, but within a generation all Taínos were dead.

In the 1880s Manuel de José Galván resurrected the story in his epic novel, *Enriquillo*, which sought to cast the *cacique* as an archetypal 'noble savage' and a Christian hero. At the time, the Europeanized Dominican elite was trying to downplay the African and Haitian roots of the country's cultural identity. Enriquillo hence stood for a non-African racial past, which could be used to explain the country's mixed ethnic roots. An implausible myth grew up that coloured Dominicans – even black ones – were not African-descended, but were in fact 'Indians', the heirs to Enriquillo's heroic resistance. Even today, mixed-race Dominicans are sometimes described as *indios*.

Various waterfowl inhabit the area. There are 62 species of bird, 45 are native to the island, including the roseate flamingo, several herons, the stolid flycatcher and the great hummingbird. The querebebé or nightjar (*Chordeiles gundlachii*), best heard at dusk, and the cu-cú or burrowing owl (*Athene cunicularia*) may also be seen (or heard).

Temperatures are extremely high, averaging 28°C but rising at times to 50°C, with annual rainfall of only 642 mm. 106 species of plant have been identified, including 10 types of cactus. Isla Cabritos is extremely hot and oppressive around midday, so arrive as early as possible and take precautions against sunburn. Public transport runs both on the north and south shores, but there is no guarantee of travelling on (or returning) the same day. The only filling stations in the area are at Duvergé and Jaragua, en route to La Descubierta.

La Descubierta
20 km northeast of Jimaní. *Map 3, E1, p256*

La Descubierta is a pleasant and quiet town. The centre of most activity is at the public *balneario* of **Las Barías**. It is a very pretty spot and cool under the trees. The community area serves local dishes; the 1.5-litre bottles of hot sauce available testify to the closeness of the Haitian border.

Jimaní
Map 3, F0, p256

Jimaní is a spread out town of single-storey housing which swelters in temperatures of up to 50°C. It is about 2 km from the Haitian border; the space in between is a no man's land of rocky terrain crossed by an extremely hot road, which has a constant coming and going of *guaguas* and *motoconchos*, and a market selling mostly shoddy or counterfeit goods. Jimaní is an authorized crossing point for foreigners into Haiti (see Getting there, Road, page 23). The immigration office closes at 1800 (or before).

Rafael Leonidas Trujillo (1891-1961)

Benefactor, Jefe, Excelencia, Father of the New Homeland, were all titles glorifying a brutal dictator, who pulled himself up from very humble beginnings to become one of the richest men in the world. Born into poverty, he received a very basic education and the details of his early life are deliberately sketchy. It is believed he was of Haitian ancestry, but Trujillo denied his black blood and promoted the Dominican Republic as Hispanic, Catholic and white. His career took off when he joined the National Guard in 1918 during the US occupation. He received training from the Americans and within only ten years he rose through the military ranks to become chief of the armed forces, allowing him to take charge of the country in 1930 and retain power until he was shot in 1961. At the time of his death, he controlled 80% of the country's industrial production and two-thirds of Dominicans depended on his enterprises for jobs. He was a megalomaniac who built up a personality cult, adorning himself with medals and titles. Santo Domingo was renamed Ciudad Trujillo, Pico Duarte was named Pico Trujillo, even time was measured from the beginning of the 'era of Trujillo'. He held on to power with the use of repression, implemented by a vicious secret police. Political opponents 'disappeared' – they were tortured, murdered, or fed to the sharks. Anyone in government lived in fear of losing his job, reputation and livelihood. While Trujillo initially admired the Americans, he was no US puppet; he put an end to the US control of Dominican customs and replaced the US dollar with the *peso*. Eventually, he carried his excesses too far – his plot to assassinate the president of Venezuela and the murder of the Mirabal sisters, finally led the USA to lend support to his opponents. Diplomatic relations were severed, economic sanctions were imposed and Trujillo himself was assassinated on 30 May 1961.

Listings

Museums and galleries

- **Centro Cultural Eduardo León Jiménez** State-of-the-art cultural centre, Santiago de los Caballeros, p.64.
- **Museo Arqueológico Regional** Collection of Taíno artefacts found in the east, Altos de Chavón, p.85.
- **Museo de Ambar** El Conde 107, Parque Colón. Small museum with shop selling amber, larimar, protected black coral (don't buy it), local gold and pearls, p191.
- **Museo de Arte Moderno** 20th century Dominican art, p50.
- **Museo de Historia y Geografía** History of the 19th and 20th centuries in the Republic, p50.
- **Museo de la Familia Dominicana** Furniture and antiques from the 19th century in a colonial house, p45.
- **Museo del Ambar** Puerto Plata's amber collection, p67.
- **Museo del Hombre Dominicano** History of Taínos, Africans and Spaniards culminating in the modern Dominican, p49.
- **Museo de Larimar** Isabel La Católica. Examples of this lovely pale blue stone found only in the Dominican Republic, p191.
- **Museo de las Casas Reales** Colonial museum, p41.
- **Museo Hermanas Mirabal** Memorial to the family who worked and died for the end of the dictatorship, Salcedo p56.
- **Museo Infantil** Children's museum, p39.
- **Museo Mundo de Ambar** One of the best amber museums in the country, p43.
- **Museo Naval de la(s) Atarazana(s)** Recovered treasure and items from colonial shipwrecks, p42.
- **Museo Virreinal** Viceregal Museum, religious art and colonial artefacts in the Alcázar de Colón, p42.

NB - all of the above museums and galleries are in Santo Domingo unless otherwise stated.

106

There is a wide range of accommodation, from the four- to five-star, all-inclusive beach resorts run by international companies, to simple lodgings for local travelling salesmen. The cheaper all-inclusive hotels usually offer buffet food and local alcoholic drinks (rum and beer), which can get boring after a few days; you get what you pay for. In Santo Domingo the string of upmarket hotels along the Malecón, Hotel V Centenario Intercontinental, Meliá Santo Domingo and Renaissance Jaragua, are designed to cater for businessmen, diplomats and politicians and are of international standard, with business centres, elegant restaurants, casinos and conference centres. Note that five-star hotels charge an average of US$140, room only, plus 22% tax. In aparthotels, the average price is US$130 for two, but this can be negotiated down for longer stays. Business travellers can often get cheaper rates than posted by requesting '*la tarifa comercial*'. There are plenty of nice places to stay in the B-C range, which offer peace and quiet, good food and comfortable rooms in pleasant locations.

Sleeping codes

Price

LL	US$201 and over	**C**	US$41-60
L	US$151-200	**D**	US$31-40
AL	US$101-150	**E**	US$21-30
A	US$81-100	**F**	US$20 and under
B	US$61-80		

Prices are for a double room in high season, based on two people sharing. There is a 10% service charge and 12% tax on all hotel bills.

In more modest guesthouses, a weekly or monthly rate can usually be arranged. Hotels with rooms for US$10-15 will be basic with erratic plumbing and electricity; check the lock on the door. For cheap rooms in *casas de pensión*, or to rent an apartment for longer stays in or outside the capital, look in the classified section of a daily newspaper.

Santo Domingo

There are many cheap hotels around the Mercado Modelo in Santo Domingo (see page 190); those on Avenida Duarte are usually used by prostitutes.

Zona Colonial

LL Sofitel Nicolás de Ovando, Calle Las Damas, **T** 6859955, H2975@accor-hotels.com, www.sofitel.com. *Map 1, D6, p252* The conversion of the Casa de Ovando has provided the most luxurious hotel in the country, a haven of cool elegance with stone walls and high, dark wooden ceilings. 104 rooms and three suites, spacious and comfortable, with marble bathroom, TV, a/c, safe box, phone and data port. The pool overlooks the river, as do many of the rooms, small well-equipped gym, massage on request, billiards and books in the lobby bar, gourmet restaurant open for all meals. Public areas furnished with wicker chairs and sofas.

L Sofitel Francés, Las Mercedes esq Arzobispo Meriño, **T** 6859331, H2137@accor-hotels.com. *Map 1, C5, p252* A restored colonial mansion with 19 luxury rooms and lovely furnishings. The restaurant is in a beautiful courtyard and serves superb French food, expensive but recommended. Buffet breakfast and tax/service included.

L-A Hodelpa Caribe Colonial, Isabel La Católica 159, **T** 6887799, www.hodelpa.com. *Map 1, D5, p252* 54 rooms and suites in art deco style with a/c, TV and fridge. A smart hotel in a good location. Bar, restaurant, internet access.

AL El Palacio, Duarte 106 y Ureña, **T** 6824730, www.hotel-palacio.com. *Map 1, D3, p252* A colonial mansion with new extension at the rear, swimming pool, heavy wooden furniture and tiled floors. No restaurant.

AL-B Hostal Nicolás Nader, Duarte y Luperón, **T** 6876674. *Map 1, D3, p252* 10 rooms in a pleasant colonial mansion, beautifully furnished with lots of modern art for sale. Friendly, personal service. Includes taxes.

A Mercure Comercial, El Conde esq Hostos, **T** 6885500, H2974@accor-hotels.com. *Map 1, E4, p252* Renovated by the French group, Accor, to a high standard. 96 rooms with good bathrooms, phone, TV and fridge. Buffet breakfast and tax/service included. Good for business travellers with business centre and internet connection.

B Antiguo Hotel Europa, Arzobispo Meriño esq Emiliano Tejera, **T** 2850005. *Map 1, C5, p252* Built at the turn of the 20th century and lovingly restored to its former glory, complete with elegant wrought iron balconies and fabulous tiled floors from the era. 52 rooms and suites with mahogany furniture. Internet centre, travel agency and sushi bar. Meals are served in the La Terraza bar on the top floor, which has a wonderful view of the San Francisco monastery ruins and the sunset. Great value introductory rates.

B Saint-Amad, Arzobispo Meriño 353, **T** 6871447, **F** 6871478. *Map 1, C5, p252* 14 rooms in a colonial house with a/c and TV. Charming restaurant and bar area, room service, internet connection, all beautifully renovated.

B-C Conde de Peñalba, El Conde esq Arzobispo Meriño facing Parque Colón, **T** 6887121, www.condepenalba.com. *Map 1, E4, p252* Great location with bar and restaurant. Newly decorated rooms with TV, suites with balcony, interior rooms have no windows, US$10 for an additional person.

C El Beaterio, Duarte 8, **T** 6878657. *Map 1, F4, p252* 16th-century guesthouse with 11 rooms set around a courtyard with palm trees and potted plants, roof terrace and patio. Breakfast is included. A wonderful renovation with antique furniture, exquisite tiles in the bathrooms, a/c and ceiling fan. Taxi service from airport, to be booked when you make your room reservation.

E Aída, El Conde 464 y Espaillat, **T** 6857692, **F** 6889350. *Map 1, E1, p252* Very pleasant family-run accommodation. A/c rooms have no windows, rooms with fan have balcony, some rooms sleep three. No smoking. Fairly quiet at night, but record shop below may be noisy during the day. Popular, central location, and so often full. Amex accepted.

F Independencia, Estrella y Arzobispo Nouel, near Parque Independencia, **T** 6861663. *Map 1, F0, p252* Clean, convenient location. Price is for a single room. Soap and towels provided.

Some rooms don't have windows. Also has a club, bar (noisy all night), language school (across the street) and art exhibitions.

F La Llave del Mar, Av George Washington 43 esq Santomé, **T** 6825961. *Map 1, G2, p252* The hotel has 10 rooms. The restaurant has aquarium tables and live piano music nightly.

West of the Zona Colonial

LL-AL Meliá Santo Domingo, Av George Washington 365, **T** 2216666, www.solmelia.com. *Map 2, E5, p253* One of the top hotels in the city. International style for business travellers with the advantage of being on the Malecón. Lots of facilities including restaurants and nightlife. Good service.

L Barceló Gran Hotel Lina, Av Máximo Gómez y 27 de Febrero, near the Centro Olimpico, **T** 5635000, h.lina@verizon.net.do. *Map 2, C4, p253* 217 well-equipped rooms, a good restaurant, casino and internet access. Convenient for Caribe Tours terminal.

L-AL Hispaniola, Av Independencia y Abraham Lincoln, near the university, **T** 2217111, **F** 5350976. *Map 2, E3, p253* Very clean with good service, but the bedrooms and corridors are showing their age. Pleasant public areas, a pool, disco and noisy, glitzy casino.

AL-A Courtyard by Marriott, Av Máximo Gómez 50-A, Gazcue, **T** 6851010, www.marriott.com/SDQCY. *Close to the US embassy and the National Theatre. Map 2, D4, p253* Within walking distance of many places of interest. 142 very comfortable rooms and four suites of high standard, sleeping up to four. Breakfast is included. Free access to the internet in the lobby or in the rooms. Five rooms are wheelchair accessible and have appropriate facilities, including a connecting room for a carer. The restaurant serves breakfast and dinner, but there is a snack machine and delivery from outside restaurants. Facilities include a well-equipped 24-hour gym, pool, self-service laundry, safe box, fridge, coffee maker, iron and spotless bathrooms. Friendly atmosphere.

B-C Villa Italia, Av Independencia 1107 casi esq Alma Mater, near the university, **T** 6823373, hotel.villa@verizon.net.do. *Map 2, E4, p253* 25 rooms, three suites and one apartment, equipped with a/c, phone and TV; a fridge is available for extra charge. The terrace has a jacuzzi and sea view. Attractive with wooden furniture and restaurant, but the service is lacking.

C-D Duque de Wellington, Av Independencia 304, Gazcue, **T** 6824525, www.hotelduque.com. *Map 2, D5, p253* Conveniently located with 28 budget rooms with TV and fridge. Bar and restaurant.

C-D La Casona Dorada, Independencia 255 y Báez, Gazcue, near Jaragua, **T** 2213535, casonadorada@verizon.net.do. *Map 2, D6, p253* 25 rooms, some of which sleep three, with a/c and TV. Facilities include a laundry and dry cleaning, small pool, 24-hour room service and secure parking. Staff are courteous.

E Bellavista, Dr F Defilló 43, Ens Bella Vista, near Parque Mirador del Sur, **T** 5320412, hotelbellavista@verizon.net.do. *Map 2, F1, p253* Rooms are good, clean and have plenty of space.

E Palmeras del Caribe, Cambronal 1, Gazcue, **T** 3335510. *Map 2, D6, p253* Rooms are nice but small, with use of a fridge. There is a pleasant garden and adjoining café.

North to Santiago

Constanza

B-E Mi Cabaña, Carretera Gen Antonio Duvergé, Colonia Japonesa, **T** 5392930, micabana@hotmail.com. *At entrance to Hotel Nueva Suiza.* Small townhouses with kitchenettes, sleeping four. Facilities include a pool, bar and volleyball court. Music can be loud. Breakfast is served but there is no restaurant.

C-D Hotel Rancho Constanza & Cabañas de la Montaña, Calle San Francisco de Macorís 99, Sector Don Bosco, **T** 5393268, www.ranchoconstanza.com, *east of town towards Colonia Kennedy.* Modern, Alpine-style, family-run hotel with 11 rooms and one suite with kitchen. All have good bathrooms, tiled floors, TV and views across the valley. There are also 12 basic cabins, good for families, sleeping up to six. Restaurant, playground, basketball, volley ball and board games, tours arranged to the city, waterfalls and hikes up Pico de Piñon. Beautiful fruit and flower gardens.

C-F Alto Cerro, east of town, **T** 6960202, c.matias@verizon.net.do. Highly thought of with camping, hotel rooms and two- to three-bedroom villas, with a great view of the valley. Villas sleep up to seven and have balconies, kitchens with stove and large fridge in open-plan living area, TV, phone, fireplace and wall safe. Very popular at weekends, there are excursions on horseback and quad bike rental. The restaurant serves home-grown fruit and veg. Large playground for children.

F Mi Casa, Luperón y Sánchez, **T** 5392764. Seven single rooms, three doubles and one suite sleeping four, all with hot water. The restaurant serves great strawberry juice and strawberry jam.

Jarabacoa

B-C Rancho Baiguate, La Joya, **T** 5744940,
www.ranchobaiguate.com.do.   Price per person. Owned by Omar
and Estela Rodríguez, it is the place to come for adventure sports,
including rafting, tubing and hiking. Lovely countryside setting
beside river, extensive gardens, 27 rooms from standard to luxury,
hot water, good bathrooms, all meals included. Two dormitories
with nine bunk beds in each for students/groups. No TV, phone or
a/c. Unheated pool, soccer and basketball court, quad bikes, horse
riding and an adventure playground for adults. Helpful, friendly
staff and management, English spoken. Free transport into town
until 2200.

D Gran Jimenoa, out of town on Av La Confluencia, Los Corralitos,
T 5746304, www.granjimenoa.com.   Rates include breakfast and
taxes, cheaper Monday to Thursday. 28 rooms set in great location
beside the river, safe for bathing when there isn't too much water.
New, comfortable and in good condition with pool, jacuzzi, indoor
games, TV, room service. Good restaurant with river view serving
local meats. Packed with Dominicans at weekends.

E California, on road to Constanza, Calle José Durán E 99,
T 5746255.   Popular, friendly place owned by the López family. 10
simple rooms opening onto patio area with arches giving shade
over the doors, bathroom, hot water, pedestal or ceiling fan, a big
room sleeps at least five. Breakfast US$5, indoors or on thatched
patio by the pool, other meals on request, *comida criolla*, bar.
Tours arranged to Pico Duarte, horse riding, rafting.

F Brisas del Yaque, Luperón esq Peregrina Herrera, **T** 5744490.
Rooms are small but new, with good bathroom, small balcony, TV,
a/c, brick and wood décor, good furnishings and tiled floor. The

place is nicely kept and is excellent value. No food provided, but convenient location in town close to restaurants.

Santiago de los Caballeros

B Hodelpa Gran Almirante Hotel and Casino, Av Estrella Sadhalá 10, Los Jardines, on road north, **T** 5801992, www.hodelpa.com. 156 rooms and suites with a/c, mini bar and 24-hour room service. Popular with business visitors, there is a casino, pool with bar, fitness centre, internet access and two restaurants serving Spanish and international cuisine.

B-C Hodelpa Centro Plaza, Calle Mella 54 esq del Sol, **T** 5817000, www.hodelpa.com. 86 rooms and suites with a/c, phone, TV, minibar and fitness centre. Smart and modern, with a good restaurant overlooking the city. Disco club Tarari next door. No parking facilities.

B-C Matum Hotel & Casino Diamante, Av Las Carreras 1, **T** 5813107, **F** 5818415, *opposite Parque Monumento*. 47 rooms; the new ones are smart and equipped with two beds, fridge, TV and phone; the old ones still a mess. Facilities include a pool, restaurant, disco and casino open from 1630-0600.

B-D Aloha Sol, Calle del Sol 150, **T** 5830090, **F** 5830950. Smart, upmarket rooms and suites with a/c and TV. Restaurant D'Manon serves local and international food, breakfast is included. Excellent value with good service.

F Colonial, Av Salvador Cucurullo 115 entre 30 de Marzo y España, **T** 2473122. Small clean rooms with a/c and fan, bathrooms, very hot water, fridge, TV and luggage store. Friendly atmosphere.

The North Coast

Puerto Plata

D Sofy's Bed & Breakfast, Calle Las Rosas, **T/F** 5866411, gillin.n@verizon.net.do. *Look for sign of Monte Silva (if you pass El Furgon you've missed the turn) between the baseball stadium and the police station on Av Luis Ginebra, go down that street and the house is the third to last on the left.* Three rooms, a great American breakfast served on the terrace and free airport transfers if you stay a week. Popular with expats.

E Aparta-Hotel Lomar, Malecón 8, **T** 3208555. 18 large rooms with cable TV, a/c or fan and warm water. Some rooms have a balcony overlooking the sea. Good value.

E Hotel/Restaurant El Indio, Plaza Anacaona, 30 de Marzo 94-98, **T/F** 5861201. Clean rooms with fan, breakfast included. The restaurant is good value and has Mexican music on Saturday evenings. There is a patio with native plants, palm trees and hummingbirds.

F Hotel Castillo, José del Carmen Ariza 34, near Parque Central, **T** 5867267, sams.bar@verizon.net.do, *look for the red awning of Sam's Bar & Grill.* The first hotel in town, dating from the 1890s. Showing its age but friendly and very cheap. One-bedroom furnished apartments or rooms with private or shared bathroom, weekly and monthly rates available, has internet access, its own generator and hot water in the evening.

F Victoriano, San Felipe 33 esq Restauración, **T** 5869752. Central location, friendly. Rooms are clean with one or two beds, fan or a/c and cable TV.

Luperón

A-B Luperón Beach Resort, Luperón, **T** 5718303,
www.besthotels.es. Excellent value, on a lovely beach with no
other hotels close by. Comfortable rooms with a/c, TV, fridge, fan
and terrace; some connect to make a suite. Three restaurants
(Italian, Brazilian and Mexican), bars, pools and jacuzzis. Plenty of
activities including watersports, tennis, riding, cycling, table tennis,
billiards, gym and sauna, and activities for children.

F Dally, 27 de Febrero 46, Luperón, **T** 5718034, **F** 5718052.
On the main road. Eight clean rooms with fan and hot water. Good
restaurant (see page 152) with The Moon disco behind. Popular.

Monte Cristi

B Cayo Arena, Playa Juan de Bolaños, Monte Cristi, **T** 5793145,
F 5792096. Two-bedroom apartments on the beach sleeping
four, with basic bathroom and kitchen. Small pool, bar, security
and parking.

D Los Jardines, next to Cayo Arena, Monte Cristi, **T** 5792091,
hotel.jardines@verizon.net.do. Two quiet bungalows each with
two basic rooms, fan or a/c, good bathrooms, beach chairs,
parking, but no food or cooking facilities. Boat excursions to the
mangroves and Cayos Siete Hermanos, English and French spoken,
jeep and bicycle hire, owner will collect you from Caribe Tours.

E Chic Hotel Restaurant, Benito Monción 44, Monte Cristi,
T 5792316. Nice hotel with 50 rooms sleeping up to four with TV,
hot water, phone, different décor in each room. Food is good, but
the service is slow. Only Spanish spoken.

★ **Hotels with a view**

Best

- Alto Cerro, Constanza, p114
- Piergiorgio Palace Hotel, Sosúa, P119
- Blue Moon Retreat, Cabarete, p123
- Villa Serena, Las Galeras, p125
- Casa Bonita, Baoruco, p135

E-F Don Gaspar, Pte Jiménez 21 esq Rodríguez Camargo, Monte Cristi, **T** 5792477, **F** 5792206. Price depends on whether the rooms have a/c, cable TV and hot water. Tony, the receptionist, is very informative, and speaks exceptional English.

Sosúa

LL-AL Haciendas El Choco, El Choco Rd, Sosúa, **T** 5712932, www.elchoco.com. A good option for self-catering. Five villas with swimming pool and large thatched verandas, all have telephone, maid, gardener, pool service and 24-hour electricity.

A Piergiorgio Palace Hotel, Calle La Puntilla 1, Sosúa, **T** 5712626, www.piergiorgiohotel.com. Victorian-style building in lush tropical surroundings, facing the Atlantic Ocean where you can observe the breathtaking sunset. Perched on the cliffs, there is no beach, but steps lead down to the water where there is good snorkelling among the rocks. Elegant hotel, impeccable décor, all rooms have semi-circular balcony and good bathroom. Romantic outdoor dining but food nothing special.

A-B Sosua-by-the Sea Playa Chiquita, Sosúa, **T** 5713222, www.sosuabythesea.com. Offering all-inclusive rooms or room only, this hotel has one of the best views of the Sosúa bay.

Immaculate, with beautiful a/c rooms, pool and bar, and fireworks on Saturday nights during the high season. Northern Coast Diving (see page 198) on site. Good location, short walk into town.

B Club Escape, Playa Laguna, 2 km east of Sosúa, **T** 5713560, www.clubescapecaribe.com. 30-room, gay-friendly hotel in a quiet area (see also page 210). There is also a nice restaurant where all meals are cooked according to guests' orders. Managers, Kari and Arthur, are very helpful offering information to their guests.

C On the Waterfront, Dr Rosen 1, El Batey, Sosúa, **T** 5713024. 27 cabins in a quiet, tropical location with ocean-front pool, on a cliff overlooking the sea. Five minutes' walk to the beach, special rates for groups. Some rooms have a/c and hot water.

D Pensión Anneliese, Dr Rosen, Sosúa, **T** 5712208, anneliese.pension@verizon.net.do. Clean rooms with fridge. Short walk to the beach. Next to On the Waterfront hotel and restaurant, see above.

E Voramar, on the outskirts of Sosúa next to Playa Chiquita, **T** 5713910, www.voramar-sosua.com. 20 rooms and several apartments all decorated in Spanish style, with fans or a/c and TV. Tropical garden, pool, tennis courts, restaurant and a pool bar. Many languages spoken.

___

Cabarete
Low-rise hotels, condos and guesthouses line the 2-km bay. Some of them offer meal plans, but there are certainly plenty of other places to eat. The largest all-inclusives, **Barceló Punta Goleta** (www.barcelo.com), **Tropical Goleta** (www.tropicalclubs.com) and **Viva Wyndham Tangerine** (www.vivaresorts.com) are to the west of town, while the smaller **Tropical Casa Laguna**

(www.tropicalclubs.com) is in town. There are two high seasons: December to April and then mid-June to mid-September when the winds are strong for windsurfing and kiteboarding.

L-B Palm Beach Condos, **T** 5710758, www.cabaretecondos.com. Spacious, deluxe condos with two bedrooms, two bathrooms, fully-equipped kitchens and patios with ocean views. Perfect for families, nannies are available. There are also studios for couples. Set on the beach in a central location, but quiet with no noise from traffic. Close to main restaurants and shops.

AL Natura Cabañas, **T** 5711507, www.naturacabana.com. Hidden away in gardens in Perla Marina, between Sosúa and Cabarete. Seven ecological thatched *cabañas* made from palm and bamboo, sleeping two to six. Each one is different in style, with hammocks on the porch. Rates include airport transfers, breakfast, taxes and a daily maid service. Spa, massages and yoga offered beside the small beach.

AL-B Bahía de Arena, **T** 5710370, www.cabaretevillas.com. Nice villas and apartments within walking distance of Cabarete. Central area with pool and jacuzzi, tennis court, convenience store, fruit and vegetable market and Swiss restaurant. Spanish, English, French and German spoken.

AL-C Velero Beach Resort, Calle La Punta 1, **T** 5719727, www.velerobeach.com. Luxurious hotel right at the east end of the beach. Rooms and suites can be combined to make apartments sleeping up to six, all with sea view, kitchen, pretty gardens and small pool. There are places to eat within walking distance. Excellent value out of season.

A-E Kaoba, **T** 5710300, www.kaoba.com. Across the road from the beach, good location and good value. Bungalows, rooms, suites and apartments at a wide variety of prices and level of comfort. All have fan or a/c and hot water. Discounts for stays over two weeks. Some of the more expensive rooms have 24-hour free ADSL internet connection for your laptop, but there is also an internet café, pool, garden, restaurant and bar.

A-E Kitebeach, **T** 5710878, www.kitebeachhotel.com. 30 rooms from budget to superior and eight apartments with a/c and balcony. Buffet breakfast included. Good value with special rates for long stays. An ideal place for kiteboarders; packages include kiteboarding lessons, kite storage, repair and cleaning facilities. There is a pool, beach bar and free internet access. Cash only, no credit cards accepted.

B-C Aparthotel Caracol, **T** 5710680, www.hotelcaracol.com. 50-room hotel at the western entrance to Cabarete, five minutes' walk from town, with studios, one- and two-bedroom apartments, all with kitchenette. Full range of services with internet access, Iguana Mama tour desk, Tropicoco restaurant, free newspapers, massage centre, TV room, children's playground and pool, babysitting and ice cream parlour. Quiet with good service and excellent value. Price includes breakfast and a kiteboarding lesson at the school on site.

B-C Windsurf Resort, **T** 5710718, www.windsurfcabarete.com. 60 one- and two-bedroom apartments. Units are spacious and luxurious, excellent value for money, all with full kitchens and balconies facing the pool. Its beach centre offers free equipment to guests staying at the resort: windsurfing equipment, surf boards, boogie boards, kayaks and sailboats. Italian restaurant, bar, evening entertainment and outings.

C-D Blue Moon Retreat, Los Brazos, **T** 2230614, www.bluemoonretreat.net, *20 mins from Cabarete on the mountain road to Moca.* Set in 38 acres of peaceful, lush, rolling farmland with a stunning view of the sea. Four simple but stylish bungalows with four suites, one family suite and one large apartment with two bedrooms, two bathrooms and kitchen. All have distinctive décor, hot water, fan and spacious living area. Small library, patio, laundry service, deluxe complimentary country breakfast, full service bar, back-up battery system and generator. Ideal for workshops, retreats and seminars. The restaurant is excellent, see page 154 for further details.

C-E Kitexcite Beach Hotel, **T** 5719509, www.kitexcitebeachhotel.com. 20 spacious rooms on Kite Beach with fans, a/c, cable TV, internet access, breakfast included. Dedicated kiteboarding hotel with kite school on site with 10 instructors, six assistants and lots of gear for rental or purchase. There is a pool, beach bar and restaurant with plenty of vegetarian options.

C-F Cabarete Surfcamp, **T** 5710733, www.cabaretesurfcamp.com. In a quiet location on the lagoon. Every kind of accommodation available at reasonable prices, from campsites and basic cottages, to more luxurious apartments with kitchens. Breakfast and evening meal can be included very cheaply. Pool, garden, terraces and internet access for laptops.

D-F Residencia Dominicana, **T** 5710890, www.hispaniola.com/res-dom. Excellent value, 24 comfortable studios, some with kitchenettes, three apartments with balconies, pool, tennis courts and own generator. Breakfast buffet, evening restaurant for dinner and snacks. Special rates for long stays.

Río San Juan
Several large all-inclusives have been built, offering lots of facilities:
Bahía Príncipe Río San Juan, www.bahia-principe.com;
Caribbean Village Playa Grande, www.occidentalhotels.com; and
Occidental Allegro Playa Grande, www.occidentalhotels.com.

E Bahía Blanca, Gastón F Deligne 5, **T** 5892528,
bahia.blanca.do@verizon.net.do.   Lovely location right on the
rocks above the sea, 75 m from the beach. A three-storey,
well-maintained, white building with 21 rooms opening out onto
balconies with a great view of the fabulously clear water below.
Rooms have hot water with good water pressure, but no TV or
a/c. Restaurant open for breakfast and dinner; meal plans
available. No evening entertainment but there are bars and a
disco nearby.

F La Casona, Duarte 6, **T** 5892597.   This is a small, exceptionally
clean, good-value hotel with hot water, cable TV, mini fridge and
purified water. Friendly atmosphere. The restaurant is famous for
its *empanadas* and fresh juices.

Samaná Peninsula

Samaná

L Gran Bahía, on the coast road, 8 km east of town, **T** 5383111.
www.occidentalhotels.com/occidentalgranbahia.   This charming,
luxury, all-inclusive resort has 110 rooms and eight villas. Good
food and service. Small beach, pool, compact nine-hole golf
course, watersports, tennis, horse riding, heliport and shuttle
service to Cayo Levantado.

B-C Tropical Lodge, on Malecón heading east, **T** 5382480, www.tropical-lodge.com. 17 rooms with hot water, fan or a/c, some have balcony and cable TV. The lodge has its own generator. It is pleasant, not fancy, but clean and has a good restaurant and pizzeria, pool and jacuzzi. Breakfast is included, other meal plans available, tax and service also included.

B-F Bahía View, Av Circunvalación 4, **T** 5382186, asavachao@aol.com. *By the middle traffic circle.* A new building with a view of the bay and within walking distance of everywhere. 10 clean and newly painted rooms sleeping up to eight; some have a/c, others ceiling fans, all have hot water. Rooms facing the harbour have a balcony. There is a restaurant on the first floor, generator and parking.

F Docia, overlooking La Churcha, **T** 5382041. New, basic lodgings with hot water and fans. Rooms upstairs have bigger windows and are lighter and brighter with more breeze; great harbour views from the balcony.

Las Galeras

Water is brackish here so you should not drink water from the tap. All hotels have saltwater showers.

AL-A Villa Serena, **T** 5830000, www.villaserena.com. Plantation house theme with wooden balconies and verandas, overhanging roofs and a charming double staircase to the lobby. The view is superb. The 21 elegant rooms have high ceilings and are all tastefully and individually furnished, with a/c and ceiling fan; each bathroom has its own water heater. Drinking water is provided and breakfast is included. Restaurant offers European-style food, including home-made pasta. Tours can be organized, free bicycles, snorkel gear for hire.

AL-C Club Bonito, **T** 5380203, club.bonito@verizon.net.do. *The first hotel on the right along the beach track, orange building.* 21 huge, luxury rooms with large balcony and sea view. Each has one or two beds, a spacious bathroom, safety box, hot water and a/c, some have jacuzzi and fridge. Large pool and lots of secluded places to sit. Reception area has a TV with video and books. Breakfast is included. The restaurant serves fresh pasta; meal plans available.

AL-C Plaza Lusitania, **T** 5380093, www.plazalusitania.com. 10 suites and apartments for self-catering. Suites consist of one huge room with bed, comfortable chairs, kitchenette, dining table, tiled floors, a/c, fan and hot water. The apartments are huge, sleeping four, with bedroom, living room with a sofa bed, kitchen area and bathroom. Conveniently located above the shops in the centre of the village.

B Todo Blanco, **T** 5380201, todoblanco@hotmail.com. Plantation house style hotel, all painted white. Eight light and airy rooms with good-sized bathrooms and balconies overlooking the sea through palm trees. The gardens slope down to the beach. Tours available.

C El Marinique, **T** 5380262, www.elmarinique.com. Two deluxe apartments, three cottages and one room set in gardens with a path down to the sea. All have fans, 24-hour electricity and include continental breakfast. The room has two beds and a bathroom, simple but adequate, with cold water. Cottages have one or two beds plus table and chairs. Apartments have a full kitchen with fridge freezer, hob and oven, a shower room downstairs, sofa bed in the living area and loft room upstairs with pine furniture and large balcony with sea view. There is secure parking and guard dogs. The food is excellent, see Eating, page 157. Fishing, horse riding and boat trips can be arranged. Internet access, meal and activity packages available.

D Casa ¿Por Qué No?, Main St.   Contact is by fax at the Communications Centre around the corner, or just turn up. Bed and breakfast, other meals are available on request. The chef specializes in seafood and oriental dishes. Two small rooms with bathroom using rain water rather than brackish water, opening onto patio and garden. The house is set back from the road in pleasant gardens and is very peaceful. Only open when the French-Canadian owners are in residence (mid-Oct to end Apr).

Las Terrenas

A Las Casitas Playa Perdida, Loma Bonita, at the end of Playa Las Ballenas, **T** 8733035, www.casitasplayaperdida.com.   Four very nice French-owned bungalows on a hillside with a sea view. Each has a loft, terrace, jacuzzi, hammocks and deckchairs. Pool, patio bar and beach. Breakfast is included and is served at the poolside or in your room. Children are catered for.

A-D Playa Colibrí, Francisco Caamaño Deñó, west end of Las Terrenas, **T** 2406434, www.playacolibri.com.   45 studios, one- and two-bedroom apartments with kitchenettes and sea view. Some sleep six to eight with daily, weekly or monthly rates. All facilities are comfortable, clean and new. Pool, jacuzzi and parking.

B-C Tropic Banana, Francisco Caamaño Deñó, **T** 2406110, hotel.tropic@verizon.net.do.   One of the oldest hotels on the beach strip, 27 a/c rooms with TV, minibar and balcony. Facilities include internet access, tennis, coaching available, lots of sporting activities, pool, good value food and a popular bar with live merengue nightly.

B-D Las Cayenas, Francisco Caamaño Deñó, **T** 2406080, lascayenas@yahoo.fr.   Nice hotel run by a Swiss-French lady.

Rooms are available with or without a balcony. Breakfast is included and is served on the terrace. There is a large room for four, which is good value.

C Las Casitas, behind Casa Nina, **T/F** 2406668, lascasitaseneljardinsecreto@yahoo.fr. Four restored Dominican houses in a quiet location with nice garden. The owners are Spanish and French.

C-D Kari Beach Hotel, at end of west track to beach, **T** 2406187, www.karibeach.com. Italian-owned. Rooms vary in price, but all are clean and have hot water. There are some large rooms with balcony and sea view. Good food. Excursions can be provided.

D Aloha, Calle Italia, just off the beach road at the Pueblo de los Pescadores, **T** 2406287, www.samana-lasterrenas.com/aloha. A quiet, clean place with hot water and a beautiful garden, run by a Spanish woman. The staff are cheerful and breakfast is included.

E Casa Nina, Av 27 de Febrero, **T** 2405490, casanina@verizon.net.do, *turn right for 800 m along the beach in Las Terrenas in the direction of El Limón.* In a nice spot, facing the sea, the renovated cabin accommodation is very cosy.

E El Rincón de Abi, El Torcido 2, **T** 2406639, dtaza@hotmail.com, *100 m inland, take turning by Pizzería Casa Coco.* Set in a quiet neighbourhood, family-style guesthouse with six rooms. Kitchen facilities for guests. Breakfast is included, and meals are available for US$6-10. Friendly atmosphere. French and English spoken.

E-F Paraíso, Av Franciso del Rosario Sánchez 53, **T** 5382648, hotel.paraiso@verizon.net.do. 200 m from the beach with a big swimming pool. Paraíso is safe, helpful, quiet and very clean.

F Fata Morgana, **T** 8365541, editdejong@hotmail.com. *Near French school off Fabio Abreu, inland between Las Terrenas and Playa Bonita.* This is a quiet place and budget option for travellers. The rooms sleep one to four people, with bathroom. There is a kitchen, book exchange, barbecue area and a large garden.

Playa Bonita

B Atlantis, **T** 2406111, www.atlantisbeachhotel.com. Veronique and Gérard Prystasz run this beach hotel, known for its excellent French cuisine; the chef used to work for President Mittérand. Rooms are spacious with marble bathrooms, some with a/c. Nice garden with coconut palms. Breakfast included.

C-D New Acaya, Playa Bonita, **T** 2406161, www.nuevo-acaya-hotel.com. 24 rooms in two buildings on the beach, all with ocean view, hot water, fan and terrace. The thatched restaurant serves a good breakfast and international menu.

E Casas del Mar, Emilio Prud'homme, **T** 2406617, supercatherina@tiscali.fr. Run by a French woman, Mme Catherine, there are eight rooms with fan and hot water. Breakfast included.

The Southeast

Boca Chica

Conveniently located within easy reach of the capital and airport, visitors tend to stay for short breaks, sometimes only a night. The cheapest guesthouses are away from the beach by the *autopista*.

A-D Costalunga, Av del Sur 3, **T** 5236883, www.costalunga.net. Italian-run, clean and excellent value; a short walk from the beach. Facilities include a/c, TV, fridge, cooker, wall safe, parking, pool, restaurant, travel agency and fax service. There is a security guard at night but no one to check you in if you arrive late.

C-D Calypso Beach Hotel, Caracol esq 20 de Diciembre, **T** 5234666. 40 well-kept rooms with a/c and TV, some of which overlook the small pool. Not on the beach, but close to it with pleasant surroundings and lots of plants and billiard tables. Small bar and restaurant.

C-D Mesón Isabela, Calle Duarte at eastern end of town, opposite Neptuno's restaurant, **T** 5234224, www.mesonisabela.com. Rooms and studios available, some with a/c and cookers. Quiet family atmosphere with personal service. Breakfast and light lunches are provided on request. Pool, bar and lounge with TV.

C-D Villa Sans Souci, Juan Bautista Vicini 48, **T** 5234461, **F** 5234327. *Three blocks from the beach.* Rooms available with or without a/c. There is a bar next to the pool, and restaurant serving excellent French-Canadian food. Prices include tax. Airport transfers can be arranged with advance notice.

C-E La Belle, Calle Juan Bautista Vicini 9, on corner of highway, **T** 5235959, **F** 5235077. A very nice place with a/c, pool, TV, bar and restaurant. Permanent water and electricity. However these may be turned off in the low season when it's quiet.

E-F Pensión Alemania, Calle 18, **T** 5235179. *Six blocks from beach.* A quiet place which is clean and good value. Small rooms, double rooms and apartments with kitchen available. English and German spoken. Airport transfers can be provided. Small pool.

Juan Dolio

All the large hotels are all-inclusive and offer pools, sports facilities, restaurants, bars and entertainment. East of Juan Dolio is the resort of Villas del Mar and the beach area of Playa Real, with eight all-inclusive resorts. There are also several apartment developments.

B-C Playa Esmeralda, Paseo Vicini, **T** 5263434, www.hotel-playaesmeralda.com.   All-inclusive with nice gardens and pool. It is quiet and low key, but the beach can get busy at weekends with Dominicans from the capital. Price per person. Diving available at extra charge.

C-D Ramada Guesthouse, on the poor road between the beach and highway, **T** 5263310, **F** 5262512.   *Opposite Marco's restaurant and bar.*   Facilities include a pool, disco, bar and watersports.

C-D Sol-y-Mar, Calle Central 23, **T** 5262514.   French-Canadian-run hotel with very clean big rooms and its own beach. Staff are helpful, but the restaurant is overpriced. Breakfast is included.

Bayahibe

There are half a dozen all-inclusive hotels along the coast and more are planned. It is more fun to stay in the village. There are *cabañas* for rent, for as little as US$10, ask around, but don't expect hot water.

L-AL Wyndham Dominicus Palace and **Wyndham Dominicus Beach Hotel**, **T** 6878583, www.vivaresorts.com. The Palace is four-star and the Beach three-star. Each has its own beach, but share facilities. There are 860 rooms and suites in total, sleeping up to four. Wheelchair accessible and adjoining rooms available. All-inclusive with many restaurants, both buffet and à la carte (reservations required two days in advance), bars, disco, theatre, diving (extra charge), kids' club, tennis, archery, soccer and lots of watersports.

B Cabana Elke, Playa Dominicus, **T/F** 6898249, www.viwi.it. Behind Wyndham Dominicus Beach, with access to their grounds on purchase of a US$40 day pass. Standard rooms have a small bathroom and can be joined to make an apartment. Apartments look onto the garden and pool, have a large living area with sofa bed, kitchenette, shower room downstairs and loft bedroom upstairs. Restaurant and bar. Discounts in low season.

C-F Boca Yate, Av Eladia Bayahibe, **T** 6886822, bocayate@hotmail.com or Daniel.muller69@wanadoo.fr. Other side of the road from Wyndham and 100 m from the Dominicus beach, day passes are available for use of their facilities. Cheaper weekly rates. Nicely painted, spacious rooms with good-sized bathroom, set around the central garden. Bar and seafood restaurant on site, specializing in lobster, open 1800-0100; meal plans available.

F Hotel Bayahibe on the main street, **T** 8330159, **T** 2245804 (mob), hotelbayahibe@hotmail.com. The best low-budget option in the village, but often full. Some rooms have two beds, TV, fridge and kitchenette (a bargain if there are four of you), bathroom, hot water, reasonable showers, a/c or fan, and balcony. Handy location for the sea and dive boats. Internet access available for US$2 per hour.

F Llave del Mar, on the main street, **T** 8330081. Newly painted in 2004, bright pink, blue, green and white, you can't miss it. There is a *cambio* and phone centre downstairs. Basic but adequate. 25 rooms with one or two beds, fan, fridge, a/c, pine furniture, small bathroom, hot water and TV.

Bávaro

LL-AL Barceló Bávaro Beach Resort, Playa Bávaro, **T** 6865797, www.barcelo.com.   A collection of five hotels, of which the **Palace** is five-star and the others four-star. **Beach** is the largest and most lively, with constant entertainment and noise, but with a wide expanse of palm-shaded sand. **Caribe** is similar but a little quieter. **Golf** is much quieter, with 126 apartments around the golf course, and **Casino** is for die-hard gamblers with suites as well as rooms overlooking the golf course. There are several themed restaurants as well as buffets, golf, a 24-hour casino, casino show, disco, Convention Centre, shops, watersports and diving (at extra cost). Beach can be full at any time of year, but Casino and Golf usually have space.

AL-A Alisios Bávaro, Playa Cortecito, **T** 6881612, central reservations **T** 5710725, info@tropicalclubs.com.   A deceptively large hotel with 97 rooms. 12 rooms are on the beach, where there is a bar open 1000-1700, snacks, massage, play area with nanny for small children, dive centre, fishing, bicycles, hobie cats, banana boat rides and beach volleyball. The other apartments, suites and large rooms are around the pool, and have a/c, mini fridge, safety box and good bathrooms. The restaurant serves Mexican and Thai food. Breakfast is included, or you can opt for all-inclusive.

B-C Cortecito Inn, Playa Cortecito, **T** 5520639, www.hotelcortecitoinn.com.   On the other side of the road from the Capitán Cook restaurant (see page 160), next to the supermarket. Centrally located and steps away from the beach, yet the pool, bar and restaurant remain quiet and secluded. Rooms are large, with two double beds, TV, a/c, fan, balcony, fridge, tiled floors and a reasonable bathroom. Breakfast is included, good value. One of the few places that isn't all-inclusive.

The Southwest

Las Salinas

AL-D Hotel Salinas, Puerto Hermoso 7, Baní, **T** 3468855, www.hotelsalinas.com. Prices are per person, rates are all-inclusive but meals are à la carte. A very relaxed terracotta-coloured hotel with 40 rooms, some on the waterfront. Rustic open-air restaurant. Rooms and suites are new, comfortable, with good bathrooms and there is an internet café. Great for windsurfers (bring your own equipment) and fishermen, many guests arrive in their own boat and tie up at the jetty (where there is also a helipad), diving can be arranged with local boatmen but bring your own gear.

D Boca Canasta Caribe Beach Club Hotel, Boca Canasta, **T** 2230664, www.boca-canasta-caribe.de. Run by Hans Dieter Riediger, this 40-room hotel is situated on the beach. Facilities include a/c, hot water, café, bar, restaurant, massage room, diving, tennis, basket and volleyball, fishing, horse riding, windsurfing, sailing, waterski, jetski and car hire.

Barahona

E Caribe, Av Enriquillo, opposite Hotel Guaracuyá, **T** 5244111. All rooms have private bath, telephone, cable TV, fan, a/c, breakfast included. Excellent open-air restaurant (La Rocca) next door.

E El Gran Marquíz, Carretera Paraíso 3, **T** 5245030/5246736. Very good value, the hotel is large and clean with rooms from one to three beds, all with private bath with hot water, fan, a/c, telephone and cable TV. Secure parking and a great restaurant. Breakfast included.

E Guaracuyá, opposite Hotel Caribe, **T** 2330748. On its own beach near the town centre. Rather gloomy, but good value, with a/c.

Quemaíto

C-D Hotel Quemaíto, Carretera Paraíso, **T** 2230099, *about 500 m down a dirt road on the left-hand side leaving Barahona.* The Swiss-owned hotel sits on a cliff about 30 m above the water and has stunning views of a small inlet below and sprawling green lawns. Some rooms have small terraces and a/c. Breakfast and dinner are included with most room prices.

C Pontevedra, Carretera Paraíso in Arroyo, **T** 3418462. The hotel is new and modern looking. Rooms have a/c, TV, hot water and include breakfast. Beach access, but the waves are very strong.

Baoruco

L-B Barceló Bahoruco Beach Resort, **T** 5241111, www.barcelo.com. An all-inclusive resort with 105 large rooms in five blocks around the pool, all with sea view and tastefully decorated, and with heavy wooden furniture. The beach is stony and the waves are rough, but a sunbathing area has been created with sun beds and thatched umbrellas. Only one restaurant, serves buffet food.

B-C Casa Bonita, Carretera de la Costa Km 16, **T** 6960215, www.casabonitadr.com. On the hillside overlooking the coast with a wonderful view from the restaurant. 12 rooms in bungalows with gardens, small pool, fan and a/c, but no TV or phone. The restaurant is expensive. Come here for relaxation rather than for creature comforts. Very popular on Dominican holidays.

Enriquillo

F Juan José, **T** 5248323. One of a couple of small, basic places to stay if you are stuck in the area after a day of drinking rum and eating fish on the beach. Part of a family home and very basic, catering mostly for Dominicans.

La Descubierta

B-D Casa Maguey, Padre Billini 26, **T** 4406060. Alex Ramírez is the owner and a major community figure in La Descubierta; although he lives in Santo Domingo, he is the perfect source for information and help. Casa Maguey is a rustic four-bedroom (all with a/c and bathroom) house with a large balcony overlooking Lago Enriquillo. Set in a large, several-acre property, it might require a little spring cleaning and visitors are expected to provide supplies, such as soap, toilet paper, and towels. Two of five basic cabins have been constructed, as has an industrial kitchen for group activities.

F Plaza Comercial Las Barías, Padre Billini 18, **T** 7514676. A small, tidy little family *pensión* conveniently located near the centre of town. A small *colmado* is also part of the house.

Eating and drinking

Like most Caribbean cooking, local food tends to be calorific and spicy. The usual starches, rice, yams and plantains, underpin most meals, while chips/fries are usually also available. Dominicans like their food well seasoned, so sauces include a good deal of garlic, pepper and oregano. The staple of *comida criolla* (Creole cooking) is the dish known as *bandera dominicana* (the Dominican flag), a colourful arrangement of stewed beef, rice, plantains and red beans, which is actually rather unspicy. More exotic and challenging is the legendary *sancocho* or *salcocho prieto*, a hearty stew made of six or seven different types of meat as well as vegetables. Even traditional Dominican breakfasts can be a serious affair. The dish *mangú* is mashed plantain, drizzled with oil and accompanied by fried onions. *Mofongo* are balls of fried plantain and pork. Goat meat is a great favourite and usually comes either as roast (*chivo asado*) or stewed (*chivo guisado*). A *locrio* is a rice dish, accompanied by meat, chicken or sausages, and the formidable *mondongo* is a tripe stew.

Eating codes

¶¶¶	US$21 and over	
¶¶	US$11-20	
¶	US$10 and under	

Prices refer to the cost of a main course. Service is usually 10%.

Another local speciality is the *asopao*, somewhere between a soup and a pilau-style rice dish (sometimes unappetizingly translated as soupy rice) which is served with fish or chicken. The ubiquitous street snacks such as *pastelitos* (pasties or turnovers filled with minced beef, chicken or cheese) are fried according to demand, as are *quipes* (cracked-wheat fritters with a meat filling) or *platanitos* (hot plantain crisps). *Tostones*, twice-fried slices of plantain, are often served as a side dish. Most Dominican restaurants assume their customers to be carnivorous and the number of vegetarian restaurants is limited. Fresh fruit is plentiful all year round and changes according to the season. *Lechoza* (papaya) is commonly served at breakfast, as is *guineo* (sweet banana). More unusual are *jagua* (custard apple), *caimito* and *mamey*. Many *cafeterías* serve delicious fresh milk shakes (*batidas*), made out of any of these fruits, water and milk (optional, *con leche*).

Drink

Statistics reveal that Dominicans account for one of the world's highest per capita consumptions of alcohol; a look around any corner store (*colmado*) will confirm this fact. The Presidente brand of lager beer comes in two sizes (*pequeño* or *grande*) and seems to enjoy a near monopoly. Other beers such as Quisqueya and Bohemia are much less visible. *Mamajuana* is a home-made spiced rum mixed with honey and sweet wine, sold in markets and on street corners. There are many rums (the most popular brands are Barceló, Brugal and Bermúdez). Light rum (*blanco*) is the driest and has the highest proof, usually mixed with fruit juice or other soft drink (*refresco*). Watch out for cocktails mixed with 151° proof rum. Amber (*amarillo*) or gold (*dorado*) is aged at least a year in an oak barrel and has a lower proof and more flavour, while dark rum (*añejo*) is aged for several years and is smooth enough, like a brandy, to be drunk neat or with ice and lime. Brugal allows visitors to tour its bottling plant in Puerto Plata, on Avenida Luis Genebra, just before the entrance to the town, and offers free daiquiris. In a disco, *un servicio* is a half-litre bottle of rum with a bucket of ice and *refrescos* (soft drinks). In rural areas this costs US$3-4, but in cities rises to US$15. Wine is imported and often mediocre and pricey, but locally produced drinks are extremely cheap. Despite being a major coffee-producer, the country does not always offer visitors good coffee, and much of what is served in hotels is either American-style watery instant or over-stewed and over-strong. Good coffee is available in small *comedores*, *cafeterías* and even from street vendors, who sell a small, dark shot for a few pesos.

Santo Domingo

Many hotels have '*buffet ejecutivos*' at lunch time and gourmet restaurants for evening meals. The **Asociación Nacional de Hoteles y Restaurantes**, Asonahores, **T** 5404676, publishes a guide to the best restaurants in the capital, '*Guía de Restaurantes*'. There are numerous pizzerias, burger bars and American fast-food chains. *Cafeterías* around the Mercado Modelo serve local lunches. Throughout the city, stalls sell sandwiches, *chimichurris* (spicy sausage), hot dogs and hamburgers. Several small restaurants specialize in roast chicken, *pollo al carbón*, with a tasty *waza kaca* sauce. Opening hours are flexible. Many restaurants open around 1200 for lunch and stay open until after midnight, or until the last customer leaves, although kitchen service is limited between lunch and dinner.

Zona Colonial

Ψ₮Ψ-Ψ₮ Coco's, Padre Billini 53, **T** 6879624. *Tue-Sat 1830-2400, Sun 1200-1500. Map 1, F4, p252* Excellent food and service, menu changes daily.

Ψ₮Ψ-Ψ₮ La Briciola, Arzobispo Merino 152, **T** 6885055. *1800-late. Map 1, E4, p252* Recommended Italian cuisine in spectacular setting in courtyard of colonial house. Dine by candlelight under the brick arches or in the open air. The piano bar has live music.

Ψ₮Ψ-Ψ₮ La Résidence, Calle Las Damas, **T** 6859955. *1200-1500, 1900-2330. Map 1, D6, p252* The restaurant is at Sofitel Nicolás de Ovando and is as upmarket as the hotel, with elegant wicker furniture and beautifully presented meals. Mediterranean-style gourmet food, served to music. Very romantic.

Ψ₮Ψ-Ψ₮ Museo de Jamón, La Atarazana 17, Plaza España, **T** 6889644. *1100-late. Map 1, C5, p252* Ceiling covered with hams. Delicious selection of tapas. Not a museum but a pleasant Spanish restaurant with live music.

Ψ₮ Campo de Francia, Calle Las Damas, esq El Conde, **T** 6890583. *From 1100. Map 1, E6, p252* Authentic regional French dishes. One of several restaurants here in converted colonial buildings.

Ψ₮ La Atarazana, La Atarazana 5, **T** 6892900. *1200-2400. Map 1, B6, p252* Popular for Creole and international cuisine, good seafood.

Ψ₮ Mesón de Barí, Hostos esq Arzobispo Nouel, **T** 6874091. *1200-0100. Map 1, E4, p252* Great place for typical Dominican dishes, merengue music at weekends, unusual collection of art.

★ Best Seafront eats

- La Casa del Pescador, Cabarete, p154
- On the Waterfront, Sosúa, p154
- El Paraíso, El Valle, p157
- Casa Boga, Las Terrenas, p158
- Capitán Cook, Bávaro, p160

🍴🍴 **Mesón La Quintana**, La Atarazana 13, **T** 6872646. *Tue-Sun 1200-2400. Map 1, C5, p252* Spanish and some Italian dishes. One of several bars and restaurants in this area.

🍴🍴 **Palmito Gourmet**, Arzobispo Portés esq Santomé, **T** 2215777. *1200-late. Map 1, G2, p252* Restaurant and bar, mix of Dominican and Italian dishes, good atmosphere.

🍴🍴 **Rita's Café**, La Atarazana 27, **T** 6889400, ramaup@aol.com. *From 1000. Map 1, C5, p252* International and Dominican food in colonial setting, paella, Mexican, meat and seafood, overlooking river, credit cards accepted.

🍴 **Anacaona**, El Conde 101 esq Isabel La Católica, **T** 6828253. *1200-late. Map 1, E5, p252* Excellent location and menu, outdoor seating.

🍴 **Bariloche**, El Conde 203. *1145-1800. Map 1, E3, p252* Self-service food. Lasagne only US$1, *menú del día* US$3, huge portions.

🍴 **La Cafetería Colonial**, El Conde 253, **T** 6827114. *0730-2200. Map 1, E2, p252* Good for fresh coffee after a meal elsewhere.

🍴 **La Crêperie**, La Atarazana 11, Plaza de España, **T** 2214734. *1530-late. Map 1, C5, p252* Nice outdoor seating on the plaza.

♟ **La Panadería**, Isabel La Católica 251. *Mon-Fri 0630-2030, Sat 0700-1700, Sun 0800-1300. Map 1, D5, p252* A good place for snacks and drinks and excellent freshly ground Dominican coffee.

West of the Zona Colonial

♟♟♟-♟♟ **Fellini**, Roberto Pastoriza 504 esq Av Winston Churchill, **T** 5405330. *1900-late. Map 2, D2, p253* Mediterranean and Italian cuisine. Elegant dining.

♟♟♟ **Mesón Iberia**, Miguel Angel Monclus 165, Mirador Norte, **T** 5317694. *Tue-Sun 1130-2400. Off the map* Spanish cuisine. Excellent food and service.

♟♟♟ **Outback Steak House**, Av Winston Churchill 25, Acrópolis Center, **T** 9550001. *1200-2400. Map 2, D2, p253* Australian franchise. Serves good steaks and salads. Free soda drink refills.

♟♟♟ **Spaghettíssimo**, Paseo de los Locutores 13, entre Avs Abraham Lincoln y Winston Churchill, **T** 5653708. *1200-2400. Map 2, D2, p253* Italian, fish, seafood, meat, pasta, open-air jazz on Wednesdays, home delivery.

♟♟♟ **Yatoba**, Av Abraham Lincoln 615, **T** 5624222. *1200-2400. Map 2, C2, p253* Eclectic, nice food and atmosphere. Beautiful outdoor decoration to enjoy a moonlight dinner or if preferred there is an a/c dining area.

♟♟♟-♟♟ **Sully**, Av Charles Summer 19 y Calle Caoba, Los Prados, **T** 5623389. *Tue-Sun 1200-1500, 1900-2400. Map 2, C1, p253* Lots of seafood in Dominican, French and Italian styles.

♟♟♟-♟♟ **Vesuvio del Malecón**, Av George Washington 521, **T** 2211954, www.restaurantvesuvio.com. *Lunch and dinner.*

Map 2, F3, p253 Established in 1954, the place to go in Santo Domingo for an expensive meal. Elegant dining, Italian cuisine with seafood and pasta, as well as Caribbean specialities. Wheelchair accessible, valet parking.

♔ **Adrian Tropical Malecón**, Av George Washington, **T** 2211764. *1200-2300. Map 2, E5, p253* Good, reliable place to try local specialities such as *mofongo*, but international dishes are also available. Perched on the waterfront on the Malecón, you can dine outdoors with the sea breeze and the waves crashing beneath you, particularly attractive at night when the rocks are lit up.

♔ **Aqua Sushi Bar**, Av Abraham Lincoln esq Gustavo M Ricart, Plaza Rosa, **T** 5403116. *1200-2400. Map 2, C2, p253* Japanese and other international dishes. Baskets of orchids as part of the oriental-style decoration.

♔ **Asadero los Argentinos**, Av Independencia entre Av Abraham Lincoln y Máximo Gómez, **T** 6864060. *1200-late. Map 2, E4, p253* Excellent Argentine food.

♔ **Barra Payan**, 30 de Marzo 140, **T** 6896654. *Open 24 hours. Map 2, C6, p253* Sandwiches and tropical juices, an all-time Dominican favourite.

♔ **Boga Boga**, Plaza Florida, Av Bolívar 203, **T** 4720950. *1100-0100. Map 2, D5, p253* Spanish, good *jamón serrano* and *chorizo*, US$15-20 for a meal.

♔ **Cantábrico**, Av Independencia 54, **T** 6875101, www.restaurantcantabrico.com.do. *1100-2400. Map 2, D6, p253* Recommended fresh fish and seafood, Spanish and *criollo*. Good reputation for more than a decade.

Cappuccino Trattoria and Restaurant, Av Máximo Gómez 60, **T** 6898600. *0800-2400*. *Map 2, D4, p253* Italian-owned restaurant and café, great Italian food, suave, prices to match, Italian murals.

Chino de Mariscos, Av Sarasota 38, **T** 5335249. *1200-late*. *Map 2, E2, p253* Very good Chinese seafood, long-standing business in operation for over a decade.

Il Capo, Jardines del Embajador, Av Sarasota, Centro Comercial Embajador, **T** 5346252. *1100-late*. *Map 2, E2, p253* Italian cuisine, excellent pizza.

La Esquina de Tejas, Av 27 de Febrero 343, **T** 5606075. *0800-late*. *Map 2, D3, p253* Spanish cuisine and bakery. Famous for their sandwiches.

Les Fondues, Av Winston Churchill, esq Sarasota, **T** 5355947. *Lunch and dinner*. *Map 2, E2, p253* All types of fondue including chocolate, run by Swiss.

Mesón de la Cava, Parque Mirador del Sur, in a natural cave, **T** 5332818. *1130-1700, 1730-2400*. *Map 2, F2, p253* Good steaks, live music, dancing, great experience, very popular, reserve in advance.

Noa Noa, Miguel de Jesús Troncoso 5B, esq Feo Prats Ramírez, Piantini, **T** 5405038. *From 1200*. *Off the map* Serves international dishes, nice eclectic restaurant with VIP lounge, sushi bar and terrace for outdoor dining by candlelight or indoor restaurant with a/c.

Samurai, Av Lincoln 902, **T** 5651621. *Mon-Sat 1200-1500, 1800-2400; Sun 1200-1600*. *Map 2, C2, p253* Very good Japanese, try the Sun brunch.

‖ **Seasons**, Roberto Pastoriza 14, **T** 5652616. *From 1130.*
Map 2, E1, p253 Spanish, tapas and other international dishes.

‖ **Sheherezade**, Roberto Pastoriza 226, **T** 2272323. *1200-late.*
Map 2, D3, p253 Arabian and Mediterranean food, with
Mediterranean architecture and design.

‖ **Vesuvio II**, Av Tiradentes 17, Naco, **T** 5626060,
www.vesuviotiradentes.com. *1200-1500, 1800-2300. Map 2, D3, p253*
Italian and international cuisine, better value than Vesuvio I. Bar,
private dining room, home delivery, Italian family business, well
thought of.

‖-‖ **Lumi's Park**, Av Abraham Lincoln 809, **T** 5404755, also at
Multicentre Charles de Gaulle, **T** 4146243, Acrópolis Center,
Av Winston Churchill, **T** 9550066, delivery **T** 5404584,
www.lumispark.com. *0800-2400. Map 2, D2, p253*
The place to be, outdoor seating under canvas, 'steak park',
churrasco, excellent *mofongos*, open until dawn, also takeaway
or local delivery.

‖ **Ananda**, Casimiro Núñez de Moya 7, Gazcue, **T** 6827153.
1000-2200. Map 2, D5, p253 Cafetería style, excellent
vegetarian restaurant.

‖ **Bagels'n More**, Fantino Falco, **T** 5402263. *From 0800.*
Map 2, D2, p253 New York bagel sandwiches, soups, salads and
muffins. The only bagel place in the Dominican Republic.

‖ **Casa del Mofongo**, 27 de Febrero y Calle 299, **T** 5411121.
0900-late. Map 2, E2, p253 A long way from the centre, but
famous for its *mofongo*, balls of mashed plaintain and pork, and
other local specialities.

♟ **El Conuco**, Casimiro de Moya 152, Gazcue, **T** 6860129,
www.elconuco.com.do. *1100-1500, 1800-2400. Map 2, D5, p253*
Good value buffet at lunch time and a more extensive buffet in
the evening. You can also eat à la carte and try more exotic items
such as *mollejitas fritas en salsa de mango* (chicken's stomachs in
mango sauce), *mondongo* (tripe) or *patica* (pigs' knuckles). A
show of typical dancing is laid on at lunch and in the evening
from 1900.

♟ **France-Croissant**, Av Sarasota 82 y Dr Defilló. *From 0800.
Map 2, F1, p253* French bakery, tastiest pastries in the country,
unsweetened wholemeal bread available, small café.

♟ **Lotus Vegetarian Restaurant**, Av 27 de Febrero y Carmen
Mendoza, **T** 5353319. *1100-1530, 1900-2200. Map 2, E1, p253*
Chinese. One of the few vegetarian restaurants in the country.

♟ **Maniquí**, Pedro Henríquez Ureña in the Plaza de la Cultura,
T 6882854. *From 1200. Map 2, D4, p253* Busy at lunch time, try
the crab in coconut, vegetarian dishes.

♟ **Provocon IV**, Santiago 253, Gazcue, **T** 2212233. *1200-2300.
Map 2, D5, p253* The best place for *pollo al carbón* with *waza kaca*
sauce. Also other locations around the city.

East of the Zona Colonial

♟ **Café del Río**, Plaza la Marina, overlooking the Ozama River.
1200-2300. Map 2, D7, p253 Good place for a cold beer, near the
Sugar Cane Monument on eastern side of river.

North to Santiago

Constanza
All the food here is wonderfully fresh, with local ingredients such as guinea fowl and rabbit.

¶ **Aguas Blancas**, Rufino Espinosa 54, **T** 5391561. *1000-until everybody goes home.* Like most of Constanza, casual dining and family dining serving typical Dominican dishes. Try the *Guinea a la salsa roja.*

¶ **Comedor Gladys**, Luperón 36, **T** 5393625. *0700-2230. Menú del día* US$2.25, plenty of food and freshly cooked, fish, goat or ask for something different, pastry counter popular with kids after school.

¶ **Exquisiteses Dilenia**, Gaston F Deligne 7, **T** 5392213. *1000-late.* Specializes in lamb, guinea fowl, and rabbit dishes. For a little variety, try the mixed grill or the *cocido*, "like a *sancocho*, but better", in the words of the chef!

¶ **Lorenzo's**, Luperón 83, **T** 5392008. *0800-2300.* Excellent Dominican food, try the guinea fowl or rabbit cooked in wine, also sandwiches, pizza and pasta, most dishes under US$5.

¶ **Los Niveles**, town centre, upstairs. *1100-1600, 1800-2300.* The poshest restaurant in town, serving steak, rabbit, guinea fowl, goat and fish, most dishes US$4-6.50, wine by the glass or bottle, special events held here.

¶ **Pizzería Antojitos d' Lauren**, Duarte 17 beside the Red Cross, **T** 5392129. *0800-2300.* Casual, plastic tables, plastic cups, chicken, *sancocho*, local specialities, popular at night for pizza and dancing. Try their house speciality – vegetarian pizza.

Jarabacoa

You can buy locally-grown strawberries beside the road, but restaurants hardly ever have them.

¶¶¶-¶¶ **Rancho Restaurant**, opposite Esso station. *Open for lunch and dinner.* *Criollo* and international, good food using locally grown ingredients, belongs to Rancho Baiguate. The walls are lined with the work of several local artists (who often dine there with the owners).

¶¶-¶ **Vistabella Club Bar & Grill**, off road to Salto Jimenoa, 5 km from town, also part of Rancho Baiguate. *Open for lunch and dinner.* Pleasant setting overlooking valley and Hipólito Mejía's new country mansion, pool, bar and excellent food, specialize in goat, guinea fowl, pigeon, duck, US$5-9, or for a snack ask for a plate of mixed *longaniza*, *carne salteada* and *tostones*, great with a cold beer, popular for lunch at weekends but often quiet at night.

¶¶-¶ **El Jalapeño**, Calle Colón next to Banca Sport. *1200-late.* Recently opened by a Puerto Rican family, this funky place specializes in Mexican food and snacks. At night a small disco is located on the roof to help you digest.

¶¶-¶ **La Herradura**, Independencia esq Duarte. *1200-2300.* Probably the best place to eat in town. Soup, sandwiches, pasta, fish and meat on the menu. Rustic décor in keeping with rancho style. Live music from 2100 at weekends, with variety of local singers performing until the early hours, particularly if the gaucho owner and his cowboy friends are there.

¶¶-¶ **Pizza & Pepperoni**, Calle Gastón next to the elementary school, **T** 5744348. *1100-2400.* Small restaurant with a covered outdoor terrace, pizzas and *calzones* hit the spot late at night.

℟ **Del Parque Galería**, Duarte at Hermanas Mirabal, **T** 5746749. Favourite national dishes and international cuisine.

Santiago de los Caballeros
There are several restaurants around the monument on Av Francia and Calle del Sol, popular on Sunday.

℟℟℟-℟℟ **El Café**, Av Texas esq Calle 5, Jardines Metropolitanos, **T** 5874247. *Lunch and dinner.* The favourite of businessmen and upper-class society, at the upper end of the price range with white linen on the tables. Good for sea bass and rack of lamb.

℟℟ **Camp David Ranch**, Carretera Luperón Km 7, **T** 6260578. *Lunch and dinner. The turning is on the right, unsigned, before the El Económico supermarket. 10-min drive up a winding, paved road to the ranch.* The food quality is erratic, but the view is breathtaking across the Cibao valley.

℟℟ **Pez Dorado**, Calle del Sol 43 (Parque Colón), **T** 5822518. *1200-2200.* Chinese and international, good quality food in generous portions, very popular for Sun lunch.

℟℟ **Rancho Luna Steak House**, Carretera Luperón Km 7.5, **T** 7367176. *Lunch and dinner. At the foot of the hill leading up to Camp David Ranch.* Great steak house and piano bar with good service, wine list and views. Not recommended for vegetarians.

℟℟-℟ **Ciao Ciao**, Av María R Sánchez, Los Jardines 13, **T** 5831092. *Lunch and dinner.* Fresh home-made Italian food. Run by an eccentric, entertaining Italian.

℟℟-℟ **Il Pasticio**, behind the Supermercado Nacional. *Lunch and dinner.* Eclectic Italian place, great for late-night drinks, a time when the owner, Paolo, is frequently there for conversation.

᛭᛭-᛭ Kukara Macara, Av Francia 7 esq Calle del Sol, **T** 2413143. *1100-0300.* Rustic décor, cowboy style, lots of steak including Angus, prices up to US$20 for a huge, top-class piece of meat, also seafood, tacos, sandwiches and burgers.

᛭ Los 3 Café, Calle R, César Tolentino 38, **T** 2765909. *1200-late.* Specializes in *comida criolla*.

᛭ Olé, JP Duarte esq Independencia. *1200-late.* Serves Dominican *criollo* food and American-style pizzería. Outdoor dining under thatched roof.

᛭ Puerta del Sol, Calle del Sol12, **T** 2417588. *1200-late.* Cheap and popular with a slightly younger crowd.

The North Coast

Puerto Plata

᛭᛭ Jardín Suizo, Malecón 32, **T** 5869564. *Lunch and dinner.* Run by Swiss James and his Dominican wife, excellent food.

᛭᛭-᛭ Aguaceros, Malecón edif 32, near fire station, **T** 5862796. *1700-late.* Steaks, seafood, burgers, Mexican, tables on sidewalk, bar.

᛭᛭-᛭ Café Cito, on the highway towards Playa Dorada. *Mon-Sat 1030-2400.* Away from the hustle and bustle, jazz music, very good food, popular with the expat crowd.

᛭᛭-᛭ Hemingway's Café, Playa Dorada shopping mall, **T** 3202230. *1100-late.* Predictable nautical, sport-fishing theme. Good food and music, a/c, good service, fun at night and during the day, live bands at weekends, karaoke some nights.

¶¶-¶ **Jungle Bar**, Plaza Turisol 12, **T** 2613544. *1000-1800, later for event nights*. English-run with English menu, come here for chip butties, curry or fried breakfast, popular with expats, particularly on quiz nights.

¶¶-¶ **La Parrillada Steak House**, Av Manolo Tavarez Justo, **T** 5861401. *Lunch and dinner*. On busy road with outdoor seating, but not too noisy or polluted at night. Tasty *churrasco* and plenty of it.

¶¶-¶ **Sam's Bar and Grill**, José del Carmen Ariza 34, near Plaza Central, **T** 5867267, sams.bar@verizon.net.do. *Breakfast, lunch and dinner*. American-run, good American food, satellite TV, meeting place, notice board, internet, rooms also available, see Hotel Castillo, page 117.

¶ **Comacho**, Circunvalación Norte (Malecón), **T** 6856348. *Lunch and dinner*. Good Dominican restaurant.

Luperón
There are lots of Dominican restaurants which are best found by just walking around town. Most restaurants serve good, freshly caught fish and seafood for less than US$10.

¶ **Dally**, 27 de Febrero 46, **T** 5718034. *Lunch and dinner*. Specializes in seafood, fresh daily, good value.

Monte Cristi
Goat is the local speciality and you will see goats all over the roads. *Chivo picante* (spicy goat) is sold at roadside stands.

¶¶-¶ **Cocomar**, by the monument to José Martí, **T** 5793354. *0800-2200*. Good breakfast, if a little greasy, also lunch and dinner, meals from US$3 per person, with the top price for the *Paella Marinera* or seafood platter.

¶¶-¶ **Don Gaspar Restaurant & Hotel**, Pte Jiménez 21 esq Rodríguez Camargo, **T** 5792477, **F** 5792206. *Breakfast, lunch and dinner.* Also a disco with a variety of music and requests, good breakfast menu, eggs, *mangú*, juice and coffee for less than US$4, Dominican and Spanish dishes.

¶¶-¶ **El Bistro**, San Fernando 26, 3 blocks from the clock, **T** 5792091. *Mon-Fri 1100-1430, 1800-2400, Sat-Sun 1000-2400.* Same ownership as Hotel Los Jardines, set in lovely courtyard on a corner with big wooden doors, white furniture and rocking chairs, seating in open air or under cover, seafood, lobster, goat, as well as sandwiches, salads and pasta.

¶ **Comedor Adela**, Juan de la Cruz Alvarez 41, **T** 5792254. *Lunch and dinner.* Family atmosphere, lots of choice, good food, parking available.

Sosúa

There are several restaurants on Main Street serving international food; walk around and see what takes your fancy. There are also several eating places along the beach, with lobster tanks. For Dominican food go to Los Charamicos, where there are *comedores*.

¶¶¶-¶¶ **Morua Mai**, Main St by the turning to the beach, **T** 5712966. *1100-2400.* Varied menu that includes meat, fish and seafood dishes as well as pizza, pasta and burgers. Good selection of wines. One of the more expensive places for dinner.

¶¶-¶ **La Roca**, Main St opposite Morua Mai, **T** 5713893. *0700-2400.* Speciality seafood and fish with catch of the day, with shrimp sold by the pound, also sandwiches and Mexican food, curry and pasta. Sit inside where there are billiards and a book exchange, or outside on the terrace.

¶¶ **On the Waterfront**, Calle Dr Rosen 1, El Batey, **T** 5713024. *0800-2200*. Fish, seafood, snacks, excellent food and a spectacular sunset overlooking the sea, all-you-can-eat. Live music at weekends.

¶ **PJ's**, on corner of Main St with Duarte, **T** 5712091. *24 hours*. Burger bar, satisfying breakfasts, chef's salad and schnitzel burger for lunch, outdoor seating for people-watching.

Cabarete
Wide range of places to eat and drink, lots of beach restaurants and bars with great atmosphere.

¶¶¶ **La Casa del Pescador**, on the beach, **T** 5710760. *1200-2300*. Excellent seafood and fish including paella.

¶¶¶ **Miró**, on the beach next to José Oshay's, **T** 5710888. *1500-2300*. Excellent dinners in arty atmosphere, on the expensive side. Art exhibitions held regularly.

¶¶¶ **Otra Cosa**, La Punta, **T** 5710897. *Wed-Mon 1800-2200, around the eastern point, near Hotel Velero*. Delicious French-Caribbean food, dinner only. The place is pretty small, so book in advance.

¶¶¶-¶¶ **Vento**, on the beach next to La Casita, **T** 5710977. *1800-2400*. Owner Julia offers well-cooked Italian food and wine.

¶¶ **Blue Moon**, Los Brazos, **T** 2230614. *1200-2400*. *20 mins outside town on the way to Moca*. Reservations essential. The only authentic East Indian restaurant in the region. Well-known for feasts of up to 90 guests in thatched-roof dining area. Dinner served the traditional way with guests seated comfortably upon cushions on the floor with banana leaves as plates and the right hand as silverware. A typical feast features vegetable pakoras, tandoori or coconut chicken or fish or goat curry, spicy vegetable curries, home-made chutneys, cooling fresh salads, cinnamon-cardamom spiced rice, and a refreshing dessert.

¶¶ **The Castle Club**, 20 mins from Cabarete in Los Brazos, **T** 2230601, castleclub@hotmail.com. *1830-2300*. American-owned. Unique gourmet dining experience, private dinner parties for 4-10 guests, reservations required.

¶¶ **La Casita de Don Alfredo**, also known as 'Papi', middle of town, beachfront, no phone. *1200-2400*. Excellent seafood, large portions, don't miss *camarones a la papi*, the chef's own recipe with shrimps and spaghetti. Decorated in local style.

¶¶ **Tropicoco**, 5 mins west of Cabarete beside Hotel Caracol, **T** 5710647. *1700-2400*. Owned by José and Ute, varied menu at affordable prices. Fantastic all-you-can-eat barbecue buffet on Saturdays, fabulous Thai food Thursdays, lots of vegetarian options.

¶¶-¶ **Lax**, west side, on the beach, near La Casa del Pescador, no phone, *1100-0100*. One of the liveliest places on the beach day and night. International cuisine including a huge Mexican special and sushi. Good food and prices. Meeting place for windsurfers and kiteboarders.

¶ **Dick's Bakery**, west end of town, near La Casa Rosada grocery store, **T** 5710612. *0630-1800*. Serves the best coffee in town and fabulous breakfasts, very popular with locals.

¶ **Mercedes**, Callejón de la Loma, **T** 5710247. *1200-2200*. *In the Dominican part of town on the way to Parque Nacional El Chocó.*

There are several cheap Dominican restaurants, but this is one of the best. Try the fish of the day.

Samaná Peninsula

Samaná
The local cuisine is highly regarded, especially the fish and coconut dishes and *sancocho*.

🍴 **Bar Le France**, Malecón, **T** 5382257. *1130-late*. Café style. Open air and indoors.

🍴 **Camilo's**, Malecón, **T** 5382781. *1100-2300*. Local and not-so-local food, reasonable (accepts credit cards).

🍴 **Chino's**, on hill behind Docia. *1200-2300*. Beautiful view, run by immigrants, doing very well.

🍴 **La Mata Rosada**, opposite the harbour, **T** 5382388. *1200-2300*. French-run but lots of different languages spoken, popular with ex-pats, not always open, seafood, about US$10 per person.

🍴 **Le Café de Paris**, Malecón, **T** 5382488. *0800-2300*. Brightly painted, good crêperie, ice cream, breakfast, cocktails, loud rock music, very slow service when busy, can take a long time to get the bill.

🍴 **L'Hacienda**, Malecón, **T** 5382383. *Thu-Tue 1200-late*. Grill and bar open from 1200, the best in town, excellent specials, main dishes US$8-10.

Las Galeras

Locals eat at the mini-*comedores* on the beach at the end of the road where the *guaguas* stop, not recommended for hygiene but plenty of local colour. You can find boatmen here for trips to other beaches.

♙♙ **El Pescador**, Calle Principal, **T** 5380052. *Daily 1600-late.*
On your right as you head out of the village, look for the coloured lights and the building painted terracotta, blue and white. Spanish-owned, specializes in seafood, fish, shrimp, lobster and crab accompanied by small salad and rice. Apparently the best in town for seafood.

♙♙-♙ **Chez Denise**, Calle Principal in centre of village, **T** 5380219. *1030-2330.* French food, a variety of yummy crêpes, delicious shrimp, salads, from US$3.50. Colourful and friendly.

♙♙-♙ **Nicole's Ocean View Restaurant**, El Marinique, **T** 5380262, www.elmarinique.com. *Breakfast, lunch and dinner.* Delicious papaya crêpes, seafood caught daily and delicious home-made desserts. Nicole bakes her own bread and pastries. Also good steaks and barbecued lobster, chicken and ribs, all served on shady outdoor veranda by the bar overlooking the sea.

El Valle

♙ **El Paraíso**, on the beach, **T** 8012246 at the marine guardhouse behind. *Daily until 1800.* Small shack on the sand serving the catch of the day, cold beer, cuba libre, pina colada and *coco loco* as well as soft drinks. Choose your own fish or shrimp, caught that morning, and have it fried or baked, served with rice and salad and followed by fresh fruit. Delicious and in an unbeatable setting.

Las Terrenas

♥♥ **Casa Boga (Iñaki & Isabel)**, between Salsa and Indiana Café, in the Pueblo de los Pescadores, **T** 2406321. *1900-2300*. The best fish and seafood in town, fresh daily, nice little restaurant right by the sea, friendly, owners are Basque.

♥♥ **La Salsa**, Pueblo de los Pescadores, **T** 2406805. *1900-2400*. *On the beach near Trópico Banana.* French-owned restaurant with thatched roof, expensive.

♥ **Aubergine**, Calle Francisco Bono, next to Hotel Cacao Beach, **T** 2406167. *Tue-Sun.* Excellent seafood, fine French cuisine, pizzas and some Chinese dishes.

♥ **Casa Coco**, Calle El Portillo 42, **T** 2406095. *1200-2400*. The first pizzeria to open in town and still good, with a restaurant or home delivery for an extra charge.

♥ **Diny**, Libertad 14, beachfront, **T** 2406113. *From 0800, barbecue 1100-2300, plato del día 1200-1600.* Serves excellent breakfast with *jugos* and lots of fresh fruit. Spanish and Dominican food, serving Spanish *albóndigas* or *lentejas* to Dominican *sancocho* or *la bandera dominicana*. Also ribs, chops, steak, fish and seafood.

♥ **Herody**, Calle Principal next to Supermercado Rey. *1200-2100*. Cheap and good food, noisy but excellent Dominican food.

♥ **Hotel Palo Coco restaurant**, on main road, **T** 2406068. *Breakfast, lunch and dinner.* Spanish-run with daily menu for US$5.50 including glass of wine and dessert.

¶ **La Capannina**, next to Hotel Aligio, **T** 8862122. *1200-1400, 1900-2300.* Good Italian food with very good pizzas, large garden and nice atmosphere.

¶ **Pizzería al Coco**, Playa Bonita. *Lunch and dinner.* Good pizzas, excellent Swiss food, nice atmosphere.

¶ **Sucresale**, at the main road, **T** 8661371. *0800-1700.* French bakery, breakfast and pastries.

¶ **Tropic Banana**, on the beach, **T** 2406110. *Breakfast, lunch and dinner.* Good food, you don't have to be a hotel guest to eat here. Friday evenings sushi and sashimi with live music 2000-2400.

¶ **Une Belle Histoire**, Calle Principal, opposite Verizon telephone company, **T** 8661288. *0700-1700.* Nadine makes some very good pastries and cakes.

¶ **Veggies**, Calle El Portillo set back off the road by Casa Coco, **T** 2406131. *1800-2300.* Beautifully painted with Afro-Taíno designs, split-level, open-air setting. Vegetarian food from Mexico, India, the Near East and the Far East. Slow service but good food.

The Southeast

Boca Chica

There are beach bars and stalls (*frituras*) all along the beach selling fried fish, *yaniqueques*, sausages, and other local specialities as well as cold beer and soft drinks.

¶¶-¶ **Neptuno's Club**, east of Coral Hamaca, **T** 5234703, www.neptunosclub.com. *Tue-Sun 0900-2230.* Built over the water, with a pier. Seafood, children's menu available, reservations essential. Live music Wednesday and Saturday nights.

Bávaro

¶¶ Capitán Cook, Playa Cortecito, **T** 5520646, capitan.cook@verizon.net.do. *1200-2400*. A great restaurant on the beach with plenty of shade, or a balcony upstairs. Specialities include fresh lobster, shrimp and fish caught locally. Steak and a *parrillada* are also available for those who don't eat fish, but there are no vegetarian options. A vibrant atmosphere.

The Southwest

San Cristóbal

¶ Fela's Place, General Leger 55, **T** 2882124. *0800-2400*. A fast-food atmosphere, for cheap food, specializing in chicken.

Azua

¶ Cira, Av Francisco del Rosario Sánchez 101, **T** 5213740. *0830-2300*. Delightful outdoor restaurant with trees and flowers growing between the tables in the garden. Specializing in goat and fish, a family atmosphere and very friendly.

¶ Dilone, Av Francisco del Rosario Sánchez. Basic Dominican dishes. Cute plastic tables with chequered tablecloths and large sheltered dining area. The house specialities include goat and conch.

🍴 **El Gran Segovia**, Av Francisco del Rosario Sánchez 31, **T** 5213726. *0800-2200.* Authentic local seafood, typical Dominican cuisine, with rustic wooden seating and decoration from the sea.

🍴 **Francia**, Av Francisco del Rosario Sánchez 104, **T** 5212900. 0800-2200. Breakfast, lunch and dinner. Creole dishes, wide selection on the menu, simple restaurant with great value and lots of good traditional food.

Las Salinas

🍴 **Las Salinas**, Puerto Hermoso 7, Baní, **T** 3108141/2480308, salinas@hotelsalinas.com. *Daily 0700-2300.* A great place to stop for breakfast, lunch or dinner, serving seafood, meat, pasta, burgers, shrimp, lobster and fish at reasonable prices. Good food in lovely setting overlooking the bay, rustic décor.

Baní

🍴 **El Gran Artesa**, Sánchez 12 at the Hotel Caribani, **T** 5223871. *Daily until 2400.* National and international cuisine. The fanciest restaurant in town with artistic décor, tablecloths, flowers and a/c. Buffet and à la carte, big events held here.

🍴 **La Casona**, Nuestro Señora de Regla 16, **T** 5223283. *0800-1500.* Creole cuisine. Simple, inexpensive restaurant with big terrace, plastic tables and chairs.

Barahona

🍴🍴 **Brisas del Caribe**, at northern end of Malecón, **T** 5242794. *0900-2300.* Excellent food and service, seafood restaurant, reasonable prices, pleasant setting, popular at lunchtime.

Los Robles, on the Malecón in front of the port. Excellent for grilled meats, seafood, and *mofongo*.

El Quemaíto, Juan Esteban Km 10 on the Barahona-Paraíso road, **T** 2230999. *0800-1000, 1900-2000.* Lunch by reservation only. Dominican and Swiss cuisine in a rustic restaurant overlooking a big garden and the ocean. Quiet ambience with traditional décor.

La Rocca, next to Caribe Hotel on Malecón. Great breakfast menu, inexpensive. Serves food all day, seafood.

Punta Inglesa, Av Enriquillo 21 on the Malecón at Hotel Caribe, **T** 5244111. *0700-2300, closed Mon for lunch.* Friendly Dominican restaurant with terrace for great views of the passing action. Specializes in seafood, good value set menu.

Jimaní

Los Lagos, Duarte y Restauración. Excellent *chivo y guandules* (goat and beans), stays open late as town's main meeting place, also has disco Krystal.

The Dominican Republic comes alive at night, whether it is families taking a promenade along the Malecón in the cool air after dark or youngsters hitting the clubbing scene. Tourists who spent their days lying on the beach move into the bars and discos after dark and many beach bars can be lively both day and night, often with live music and dancing. There is a wide variety of music played, although merengue dominates and gets the hips swaying and the feet tapping. The best clubs are in the capital city, but there are many great bars in coastal areas, particularly in places like Cabarete, frequented by the windsurfing crowd. Things start to happen around midnight and go on late, usually until around 0400 but often after that.

Santo Domingo

Several of the large hotels have free live music in the evenings, from piano bars in the lobby (El Embajador) to orchestras (Hotels Meliá Santo Domingo and Jaragua). Live music in many of these hotels coincides with happy hour and is a pleasant way to get the evening's entertainment started. *Pericos ripiaos* (see page 167) can be heard at the colmados near the Malecón in Ciudad Nueva on Friday or Saturday nights. The top hotels have the best dance floors, with admission prices of US$2-10, depending on whether there is a live band or recorded music. Dominicans dress smartly to go dancing, so no jeans, T-shirts or trainers. For a list of events in local bars and clubs, see www.bonche.com and www.uepa.com.

It is not safe to walk around Santo Domingo after 2300; street lighting is not always good, so take a taxi. Sex tourism is rife in Santo Domingo and you will be taking a risk if you participate. Remember the age of consent is 18. Pickpocketing is common. In any bar or disco, unattached men will be approached by girls (*chicas*), while unattached women are considered fair game. Girls in brothels are checked for sexually transmitted diseases, but those on the street are not. For gay bars and clubs, see page 211.

Bars and clubs

Bars

Abacus, Hostos 350 esq Luperón, Zona Colonial, **T** 3337272, www.abacus.com. *Map 1, D4, p252* A great place to gather with friends for a drink. Low couches, soft lighting, good mix of cocktails, DJ music.

Alta Copa, Pedro A Bobea, Bella Vista, **T** 5326405. *Map 1, E1, p252* Former wine shop, now the place to gather with friends for a nice glass of wine or cocktails. Decorated as a *cava*.

Atarazana 9, La Atarazana 9, Zona Colonial, **T** 6880969. *Map 1, C6, p252* Colonial building, very historic, nice place, good drinks.

Beer House, Gustavo Mejía Ricart esq Winston Churchill, **T** 6834804. *From 1700. Map 2, D2, p253* Stocks about 30-40 beers from around the world, live bands (often jazz) mid-week, decent, casual ambience.

Fusion Rose, El Conde esq Las Damas, Zona Colonial, **T** 4492346, www.fusionrose.com. *Map 1, E6, p252* Hip-hop electronic music. Wednesdays hip-hop crazy nights (US$2). Popular with the young crowd.

Pop Lounge, Arzobispo Nouel esq Hostos, Zona Colonial, **T** 6865176, www.pop.com.do. *2100-late. Map 1, E4, p252* European design influences with pop art for decoration. Multicoloured cocktails and coloured ice. House and European dance music. Latest activities are posted on the website.

Praia Café Lounge, Av Gustavo Mejía Ricart, Naco, **T** 7320230. *Map 2, C3, p253* Exotic decoration, good cocktails, popular place for social activities among Dominican people.

Punto G, Paseo de los Locutores 58, Edif Gold's Gym, 2nd floor, **T** 5497675. *Map 2, D2, p253* Little place to meet with friends for a drink and appetizers.

Republic K, Paseo de los Locutores, Plaza Las Americas II, **T** 3810673. *Map 2, D2, p253* Clients must be 23 years or older.

Steak House Café, Av Gustavo M Ricart 52, **T** 5495505. *From 1200. Map 2, C3, p253* Serves good food and cocktails. Often plays music from the 80s. Happy hours from 1700-1900.

> ### *Perico ripiao*

The term *perico ripiao* has come to symbolize a type of merengue popularized and developed in the Cibao valley. In the early part of the 20th century, merengue was frowned upon by the bourgeoisie while the workers adopted it as their popular entertainment, particularly on Sunday afternoons and at other fiestas. It was associated with low life, something not quite proper, with lewd or raunchy lyrics, and took hold in the red-light districts and bars of Santiago. One of these bars was called the Perico Ripiao, or 'ripped parrot', and its name has become synonymous with the local musical genre. Since the 1970s the merengue has got much faster, with less formal steps and an electric bass instead of marimba, but the accordion is still the prized instrument in a *perico ripiao* and Santiago has produced many outstanding players with an indomitable style known as *tigueraje*.

TGI Friday, Av Winston Churchill, Plaza Acropolis, 3rd floor. *1200-late. Map 2, D2, p253* Good food. Bar area has floor-to-ceiling windows, large crowd for happy hour.

Trio Café, Abraham Lincoln 12-A, **T** 4120964. *Map 2, E3, p253* Exquisite place, good music, fine people.

XxO Bar and Lounge, Hostos esq Emiliano Tejera, **T** 6858103. *Map 1, C4, p252* Weekly activities such as hip-hop and ladies' night.

Clubs

Club 60, Máximo Gómez 60. *Fri-Sun from 2100. Map 2, D4, p253* Rock, merengue and ballads. On Friday and Saturday they play merengue and pop music, on Sundays they play Cuban *son*.

Appeals to the older crowd, most clients are over 30. US$1.

El Rincón Habanero, Sánchez Valverde y Baltazar de los Reyes, Villa Consuelo. *Map 2, B6, p253* Working-class enthusiasts of Cuban *son* dance to records of the 1940s and 1950s.

Etnia Disco, Av Venezuela, Ens Ozama. *From 2100. Map 2, B8, p253* No cover charge. Merengue and salsa for Latin lovers.

Guácara Taína, Paseo de los Indios, Av Cayetano Germosén, **T** 5330671. *2100-0200. Map 2, F1, p253* Shows of Taíno dancing in the spectacular setting of a huge natural cave with stalactites and indigenous pictographs. Also a disco with all types of music, two dance floors, happy hours and fashion shows. Capacity for 2,000 guests. US$4-12. For daytime tours of the cave **T** 5302662 (0900-1700), or **T** 5331051 (1700-2100), reserve 24 hours in advance.

Jet Set, Independencia 2253, **T** 5354145. *2200-late. Map 2, G1, p253* The place for good Latin dance music. Dress casual. Live merengue bands on a schedule basis but mostly on Mondays. Livens up after midnight.

Loft Lounge & Dance Club, Tiradentes 44, Naco, **T** 7324016, www.loft.com.do. *Map 2, D3, p253* The website lists activities and events such as live merengue, salsa and pop. Dress casual.

Maunaloa Night Club, in the Centro de los Héroes, **T** 5332214. *2200-late. Map 2, F3, p253* Live music and comedians, dancing to Dominican music. Only open when there are scheduled activities.

Montecristo Café & Club, Abraham Lincoln esq José Amado Soler, **T** 5425000. *Map 2, C2, p253* Happy hour 1700-1900. Café turns into a dance floor after midnight. Dress casual.

Salón La Fiesta, in the Jaragua Hotel, Av George Washington 367, also Jubilee, **T** 6888026. *Map 2, E5, p253* One of the top international-style hotels in the city where you can combine gambling with a little exercise on the dance floor. Dominican music.

Secreto Musical Bar, Baltazar de los Reyes and Pimentel. *Map 2, C6, p253* Cuban music, headquarters of Club Nacional de los Soneros, rock, merengue, salsa and ballads.

Seven to Seven, George Washington (El Malecón), **T** 2211919, seventosevenritmo@hotmail.com. *Map 2, F3, p253* Nice place, with merengue, salsa and pop music. Dress casual.

Santiago de los Caballeros

Santiago de los Caballeros is the home of *perico ripiao* (see page 167), a folk style of merengue, which can be heard in bars and clubs alongside more modern merengue, salsa, *bachata* (see page 179) and disco music. The Monument is always a great place to hang out. The Matum and Gran Almirante Hotels have casinos open until 0400.

Bars

Bar Code, Cuba 25, Santiago. Popular courtyard bar with live music. A pleasant place to relax with friends.

Daiquiri Loco, JP Duarte esq Oeste, Santiago. Lively, outdoor bar with snack food, including toasted sandwiches and burritos. Try one of their great frozen daiquiris.

Francifol, Del Sol esq Parque Duarte, Santiago. Pub atmosphere with ice cold beer. Not too loud for conversation.

Metropolis Billards, Estrella Sadhalá, Santiago. Bar with several pool tables, a students' local.

Tin Marín, Estrella Sadhalá esq Argentina. Lively outdoor bar popular with the young rich of Santiago.

Clubs

Alcazar, Gran Almirante Hotel, Estrella Sadhalá esq Calle 10, Santiago. *2200-late*. A popular disco which gets going around 0100 and stays full until 0700. Dress to kill. US$1.

Ambis, Autopista Duarte Km 2, **T** 5810854. *2300-late*. A long-established disco and one of the biggest in the area. Lots of girls looking for men with money to spend on them.

Tarari Disco Club, Calle Mella esq del Sol, next to Hodelpa Centro Plaza, Santiago, **T** 5817000, www.hodelpa.com. *Mon-Fri 1800-dawn, Sat from 1900, Sun from 1600*. Dancing all night until everyone goes home, live shows Tuesday and Thursday.

The North Coast

Puerto Plata

On Sunday nights there is open-air dancing on the Malecón, with huge sound systems on the road and street vendors selling drinks. Most of the nightlife is in Playa Dorada where there are discos and a casino.

Café Cito, on the main road. *Mon-Sat 1030-2400*. *On the roadside, 5 mins' walk west from the entrance to Playa Dorada.* Makes a change from the hotel complex. Bar with pool table, sports TV, live music and karaoke at weekends, very cold beer. See also Eating, page 151.

Crazy Moon, Paradise Beach Resort, **T** 3203663. *2200-0400*. Popular bar and club offers a mix of merengue, salsa and international pop music. Plenty of Dominicans to teach you how to dance and more.

Hemingways, Playa Dorada in the mall, **T** 3202230. Very popular bar at night with good mix of music and dancing, live bands at weekends, sometimes karaoke. Serves food, see Eating page 151.

The American Casino, Jack Tar Village, Puerto Plata, **T** 3201046, www.allegroresorts.com. Free drinks for players and free gaming lessons to get you hooked. Live entertainment. Disco 2300-0200, with variety of music and good lighting.

Sosúa

Britannia, Main St. *1000-2400*. Very popular bar among residents.

D' Classico, Main St. *2200-0400*. Gets going after 2300. A nice, new, big disco, mixing local and international music. From Friday to Sunday you will have the chance of meeting more locals and learning how to dance merengue and *bachata*. At weekends they sometimes charge an entry fee of US$2.

D' Latino's Club, Main St. *2200-0400*. Disco and bar, smaller than the others, but music is good. Renovated 2004. Sometimes an entry fee of US$1, depending on the day.

High Caribbean Disco. *2200-0500*. *By the casino at the east end of the town*. Closed for renovation 2004. Disco with terrace and a small indoor and outdoor swimming pool. Entry fee of around US$2 depending on the day.

On the Waterfront, Calle Dr Rosen 1, **T** 5713002. Primarily a restaurant, but a great place to watch the sunset, perched on the cliff top, with happy hour 1600-1800 when the sun goes down. See also Eating, page 154.

Voodoo Lounge, at the end of Main St. *1900-0300*. A nicely decorated cocktail bar and disco with no entry fee. Situated close to the beach, there are different ambiences including an outdoor terrace. It offers mostly an international atmosphere.

Cabarete

Cabarete has quite a reputation for its nightlife. Many of the beach restaurants double as bars in the evening and are often still open when the sun comes up. You can dance the merengue or listen to international music. Ask any local and they will point you in the direction of the party that night.

Bambú, close to Onno's. *1100-0600*. Large, comfortable club with chairs and sofas. Good place to have a drink and dance until sunrise.

Crazy Horse, behind Iguana Mama, **T** 8020914. *0900-0600*. Happy hour 2100-2300. Dancing girls at weekends.

José Oshay's Irish Beach Pub, beachfront, **T** 5710775. *Through José Oshay's Shopping Village, near Miró. 0800-0100*. Popular drinking spot which serves one food dish every night.

Las Brisas, beachfront, east side, beside Iguana Mama, **T** 5710614. *0700-0400*. Buffet-style dinners, affordable food, one of the hot spots at night. The only club where they play Dominican music, but it attracts quite a lot of prostitutes.

Onno's, town centre on the beach, **T** 3831448. *Access by Harrison's jewellers 1100-0600*. Relaxed ambience during the day but club is completely packed at night.

Tiki Bar, on the street side, opposite the Kodak photo shop. *1200-0400*. Live DJ and house music.

Village Club, next to Villa Taína, after Dick's Bakery, **T** 8020914. *2000-0300*. If you like jazz, this is your place. Live music at weekends, ask around to check who is playing.

Samaná Peninsula

Samaná

The outdoor nightlife in Samaná is to be found along the Malecón, where several stalls are set up as bars at weekends and fiestas. There is usually music at one or other of the restaurants, whether live or recorded. Nightclubs open and close sporadically and many are little more than brothels.

Las Terrenas

Las Terrenas is quite lively at weekends, particularly along the beach road, with street sellers of food and drinks and impromptu drum music, but this is not Ibiza. There is often music at the bars and restaurants for gentle entertainment.

El Mosquito, Pueblo de los Pescadores, Las Terrenas. **T** 8674684. *1800-0200*. Nice seafront bar with good atmosphere. A good meeting point.

Nuevo Mundo, Av Duarte, Las Terrenas. *2100-0300*. Popular disco although tourists pay more than Dominicans.

Paco Pasha, Libertad, Las Terrenas. Nice club but expensive.

Syroz, Libertad, Las Terrenas. **T** 8665577. *1700-0400*. Bar and dance floor on the beach with live music at weekends.

The Southeast

Boca Chica

Boca Chica has numerous small bars along Calle Duarte, which is closed to traffic at night. Restaurants stay open until around 2300 and a family atmosphere prevails. After midnight, restaurants close but bars stay open and the party starts. From around 0200 hotel and restaurant workers show up and by 0300 everything is in full swing, finally winding down around 0400. There is plenty of variety for unattached males, female prostitutes are provocatively dressed. The tourist office is trying to clean up under-age prostitution and drug abuse, with the resulting closure of several bars.

The Dominican Republic is known primarily for its rich musical culture rather than for drama or film, and has produced musicians of excellent quality, both writers and performers of merengue and *bachata*, who play to knowledgeable and enthusiastic audiences.

Live music can be found in bars and clubs all over the island, while festivals are an excuse to hold open-air street parties, often along the seafront promenade, with local and internationally famous bands.

Hotels put on music and dance displays for guests, introducing them to traditional folk music, costumes and carnival costumes and legends. The limited number of theatres put on drama, dance and opera for local audiences, often with invited Latin American artists.

Cinema

The Dominican Republic is regularly used for film locations, often standing in for Cuba, where American companies are not allowed to do business. There is a small but growing local movie industry, supported by the Government film office under the direction of film maker Luis Basanta. Two recent Dominican comedies which were locally successful are *Nueba Yol* and *Perico Ripiao*. Cinemas show the latest Hollywood releases as well as a crop of sex and violence films popular with local audiences. Ticket prices are around US$3.50. Some cinemas have discounts Monday to Wednesday at the earlier showing. Performance times are 1700-2200 in most cinemas. New releases come out on Thursdays.

Santo Domingo

The main cinemas are: **Broadway Cinemas**, Plaza Central Mall, 3rd floor, Av 27 de Febrero esq Winston Churchill, Santo Domingo, **T** 8720272 *Map 2, D2, p253*; **Caribbean Cinemas**, Diamond Plaza Mall, Av de Los Próceres, Santo Domingo, **T** 5658866, *Map 2, B2, p253*. Also at Plaza Acrópolis, Av Winston Churchill, **T** 9551010, www.caribbeancinemasrd.com; **Cinemacentro Dominicano**, Av George Washington, Santo Domingo, **T** 6888710 *Map 2, E5, p253*; **Hollywood Diamond Cinemas**, Av Abraham Lincoln, Diamond Mall, Santo Domingo, **T** 6831189 *Map 2, B2, p253*; **Palacio del Cine Cinemas**, Bella Vista Mall, Av Sarasota, Santo Domingo, **T** 2550921 *Map 2, F1, p253*.

Puerto Plata

Cine Teatro Roma, Beller 39, Puerto Plata, **T** 3207010; **Cinemar**, Plaza Puerto Dorado, Puerto Plata, **T** 3201400.

Cine Hollywood 5, Av Sadhalá 1, Santiago, **T** 9714880.

Music and dance

Music and dance is part of everyday life, an essential part of what makes a Dominican. The most popular dance is the merengue; a great many bands/*orquestas* have recorded merengue rhythms and their stars are now world-famous. Especially popular are Juan Luis Guerra, Francisco Ulloa, Wilfredo Vargas and Johnny Ventura. Salsa and *bachata* are also very popular and live music can be heard at a number of venues. For further information, see Bars and clubs, page 164 and Festivals and events, page 182.

Merengue
Merengue is believed to have developed in the mid-19th century as a local version of European dances for couples, such as contredanse. An Afro-Caribbean flavour was added with lively rhythms and lyrics to reflect social commentary. It was the music of the people, from cane cutters to dockworkers, and frowned upon by the upper classes. There would be four musicians, playing the *cuatro*, similar to a guitar, the *güira*, a cylindrical scraper of African origin but akin to the Indian gourd scraped with a forked stick, the *tambora*, a double-headed drum using male goatskin played with the hand on one head and female goatskin played with a stick on the other, and the *marimba*, a wooden box with plucked metal keys. Despite regional variations, the merengue of the Cibao valley around Santiago developed most strongly and became known as the *merengue típico*. In the 1920s, it was played with an accordion, introduced by the Germans, a *güira*, *tambora* and *marimba*. Over the years, other instruments have been added, such as the saxophone, horn or electric bass guitar. A merengue would have a

Best

★ **Bars in Santo Domingo for live music**

- Guácara Taína, page 168
- Maunaloa, see page 168
- Jet Set, see page 168
- Loft Lounge, see page 168
- Salón la Fiesta, see page 169

short introduction, *paseo*, then move into the song, or merengue, followed by a call and response section, the *jaleo*. Although similar to some Cuban or other Latin music and dance, the steps of the merengue are simpler, with a basic two-step pattern, but at a fast tempo with a suggestive hip movement.

Bachata

Bachata also emerged from the peasants and shanty-town dwellers. It was music for the soul, for the poor and downtrodden, the dispossessed farmers who were forced off the land in the 1960s and flooded into the urban slums with their guitar-based *canciones de amargue*, songs of bitterness. The traditional group had one or two guitars, maracas, bongos and marimbas, with a solo male singer, who sang songs based on the Cuban *son*, Mexican *ranchera*, merengue and *boleros*. The songs expressed the frustrations of the newly-urban male, a macho without a cause, who was often unemployed and dependent on a woman for his income. The sudden rise in popularity of *bachata* was principally due to Juan Luis Guerra, who experimented with the romantic, sentimental genre and sensitively created a poetry which appealed to everyone, particularly women. He has written songs of love (*Burbujas de amor* won him a Grammy award and is the best-selling Dominican record of all time), social criticism (*Visa para un sueño* is about visa applicants at the US embassy in Santo Domingo) and intellectual themes (*Frío frío* was influenced by Spanish poet Frederico Gracía Lorca) and is still going strong.

Ga-gá

Haitian music and dance crossed the border with the sugar cane cutters and can be seen at festival times in the *bateyes* in sugar areas such as La Romana, or in urban slums where Haitians live. *Rara* is the term used to describe the street celebrations in Haiti around Easter. Music, dance and spirit possession are all part of the rituals. The Dominican version of the *rara* is known as *ga-gá*, and is most common in the west, along the border, where *vodú* religion is practised (see page 185). *Ga-gá* bands play single note trumpets called *vaksin*, made of bamboo, which they blow and drum rhythmically with sticks and other percussion instruments (even empty beer bottles), while ceremonies take place accompanied by parades, dancing, drinking, fighting and sex. The celebrations are boisterous and audience participation is actively encouraged, but participants are expected to contribute in money or alcohol.

Theatre

In Santo Domingo the **Teatro Nacional**, Plaza de la Cultura, Av Máximo Gómez, Santo Domingo, **T** 6873191, *Map 2, D4, p253* is used for drama, dance and opera, lectures and presentations. The **Casa de Teatro**, Arzobispo Meriño 110, Santo Domingo, **T** 6893430, *Map 1, F4, p252* holds small drama workshops.

Altos de Chavón Amphitheatre, Casa de Campo, La Romana. **T** 5233333. Outdoor mock-Roman amphitheatre, which has hosted performances by international stars such as Juan Luis Guerra, Julio Iglesias, Gloria Estefan, Shakira and Santana.

Gran Teatro del Cibao, Av Las Carreras, Santiago de los Caballeros, **T** 5831150. Seats 15,000 in its main auditorium. Shows opera, merengue and plays.

Dominicans never need much of an excuse for a party and enjoy their fiestas to the full. Carnival is celebrated around the country with regional variations, and each town or village has its saint's day with processions, music, dancing and drinking, known as *patronales*. Based in Roman Catholicism, everyone gets involved and has a party. There are music festivals, food fairs and sporting events all held with great fanfare, but the biggest events are religious festivals.

January

New Year (1 January) New Year is celebrated in the capital on Avenida Francisco Alberto Caamaño Deñó (formerly Avenida del Puerto) beside the river. The major bands and orchestras of the country give a free concert, which attracts thousands of people. The celebration ends with fireworks and the whole area becomes a huge disco.

Day of the Virgen de la Altagracia (21 January) The spiritual mother of the Dominicans is celebrated with '*velaciones*', or night-long vigils, and African-influenced singing and music, found in many towns. Higüey is the site of a mass pilgrimage and huge all-night party.

February

Carnival (starting weekend before Independence Day, 27 February) Notable in Santo Domingo for the parade along the Malecón. Carnival in Santiago de los Caballeros is very colourful; its central character is the piglet, which represents the devil. Working class *barrios*, particularly La Joya and Los Pepines, have developed rival themes of Los Lechones and Los Pepines and there is much competition between them. The *lechones* have papier mâché masks of stylized pigs, while the *pepines* have pointed horns on their masks, often hugely decorated. Parades start from Las Carreras and end up at the Monumento a los Héroes de la Restauración.

On Sundays in February in Monte Cristi, the *Toros* and the *Civiles* compete against each other on the streets. The *Toros* wear costumes with elaborate bull masks, wielding whips with a ball.

La Vega also celebrates for several Sundays prior to Lent. *Comparsas*, sponsored music groups, compete for the best costumes. Materials are brightly coloured and hundreds of little bells are sown into the costumes. A typical devil's costume consists of wide trousers, tied at the ankles, a loose shirt with large sleeves, tied at the wrists and waist to make a little skirt, a cape called a *galacha* which covers the head and falls down the back, a mask to cover the face and a *vejiga* (balls traditionally made from cows' bladders) to whirl around and hit people. They can leave nasty bruises and the police have to test them to make sure they are not too solid.

Jarabacoa's carnival is similar to that in La Vega, but on a smaller scale: rather chaotic with lots of music and rum all month. See www.carnaval.com.do for further details.

International sandcastle competition   Cabarete. Visitors construct fantastic mermaids, flowers, fruit and even the Titanic.

April

Holy Week   The most important holiday time for Dominicans, with processions and festivities such as the *guloyas* in San Pedro de Macorís, the mystical-religious *ga-gá* in sugar cane villages and the *cachúas* in Cabral in the southwest.

June

Cabarete Race Week (windsurfing) and the **Kiteboarding World Cup** make Cabarete the place to be in June. The town is taken over by windsurfers and kiteboarders from all over the world, who come to compete in the tournaments. See Sports, pages 202 and 205, for further details, or www.cabareteevents.com.

July

Merengue Festival (last week July/first week August) In Santo Domingo, the festival starts with a parade of dancers and

▶ Voodoo

Vodú, the syncretic mixing of African and European religion, which stems from the import of slaves in the early 16th century. Mixing reconstructed Taíno rituals, Catholic saints and African divinities, believers worship archetypal *lúas* or gods. Ceremonies involve music, dancing, trances and spirit possession, and often take place at what are thought to be holy Taíno sites or in rural villages during their fiestas. Other well-known venues for *vodú Dominicana* are the mostly black, inner-city barrios or Villa Mella and the western mountain town of San Juan de la Maguana. A connected phenomenon is the widespread Dominican interest in *brujería*, or witchcraft. *Brujos* are thought to have supernatural powers, both benevolent and malevolent, and are consulted by a wide cross-section of the population in search of cures for all manner of ills. Market-place stalls and *botánicas* (shops selling religious paraphernalia of all sorts) testify to the country's fascination with spiritual and supernatural forces.

musicians along the Malecón and includes festivals of gastronomy, cocktails, handicrafts, art and sculpture.

Festival Presidente de Música Latina Held over a weekend every other year in the Olympic Stadium, featuring musicians from all over Latin America.

August

Restoration Day (16 August) The anniversary of the date that Spain withdrew its officials and troops and the Republic was restored. Celebrated across the country with carnival-type parades and costumes.

September

Merengue Festival (last week of September) Sosúa.

October

Merengue Festival (first week of October) Puerto Plata holds its festival along the Malecón La Puntilla.

Dominican Jazz Festival The festival in Cabarete features jazz artists from all over the world.

November

International Surf Competition Cabarete.

December

In Samaná, traditional dances, such as *bambulá* and the *chivo florete* can be seen at local festivals: 4 December, the **Patron Saint's Day**, and 24 October, **San Rafael**.

Shopping

Since the devaluation of the peso in 2003, the Dominican Republic has been very cheap for foreigners, although prices are now rising and inflation is hitting Dominicans hard. For those with foreign currency, food is inexpensive, rum and beer are very cheap and many bargains can be had when buying souvenirs. The native amber is sold throughout the country (see page 66); amber sold on the street is likely to be plastic. Larimar, a sea-blue stone found only in the Dominican Republic, and red and black coral are also available (remember that coral is protected, do not buy it). Other souvenirs are leather goods, basketware, woven goods and onyx jewellery. Paintings and other art work are on sale everywhere, but beware of the brightly coloured, mass-produced Haitian-style native art, which is low-quality and churned out for tourists. Good Dominican art is for sale in the Santo Domingo galleries or you can buy direct from artists in Jarabacoa. There are excellent cigars (see page 63), rum and coffee at reasonable prices. Bargaining is acceptable in markets but rarely in shops.

Calle El Conde, now reserved for pedestrians, is the oldest shopping sector in **Santo Domingo**; Avenida Mella at Duarte is good for discount shopping. A flea market, Mercado de las Pulgas, operates on Sundays in the Centro de los Héroes and at the Parque Mirador del Sur at Avenida Luperón.

Art galleries

Centro de Arte Cándido Bidó, Dr Báez 5, Santo Domingo, **T** 6855310. *Map 2, C6, p253*

Galería de Arte Nader, Rafael Augusto Sánchez 22, Torre Don Roberto, Ens Piantini, Santo Domingo, **T** 5440878. *Map 2, D2, p253* The Nader family are hugely influential and stock collectors' items of Haitian, Dominican and other Latin American works of art.

Bookshops

Centro Cuesta del Libro, 27 de Febrero esq Abraham Lincoln, Santo Domingo **T** 4734020. *Mon-Sat 0900-2100, Sun 0900-1500. Map 2, D3, p253*

New Horizons Book Shop, Av Sarasota 51, Santo Domingo, **T** 5334915, *Map 2, E3, p253* and 3rd floor of Bella Vista Mall, Santo Domingo, **T** 2550676. *Map 2, F1, p253*

Thesaurus, Av Abraham Lincoln esq Sarasota, Santo Domingo, **T** 5081114. *Mon-Sat 0830-2100, Sun 1000-1600. Map 2, E3, p253* Sofas, reading areas, café, play area, cultural events with Dominican authors, some English language books.

Tienda Macalé, Calle Arzobispo Nouel 3, Santo Domingo, **T** 6822011. *Open daily. Map 1, E4, p252* Wide selection of books, especially on the Republic's history.

Cigars

Boutique del Fumador, El Conde 109, Santo Domingo, **T** 6856425, www.caobacigars.com. *Map 1, E5, p252* A factory outlet for Caoba cigars on the Plaza Colón. You can have a tour of the works, seeing how cigars are made and aged.

León Jiménez Tobacco Factory, Av 27 de Febrero, Santiago, **T** 2411111. Excellent tour of the factory followed by visit to the shop. See also page 62.

Crafts

Mercado Modelo, Av Mella esq Santomé, Santo Domingo. *Mon-Sat 0900-1230, 1430-1700. Map 1, C1, p252* Gift shops, handicrafts, paintings, foodstuffs are all crammed in the market, floor to ceiling; bargain to get a good price, most prices have been marked up to allow for this. Guides appointed to assist tourists get a 5-10% commission from the vendor. There are also 'speciality shops' at larger malls. Prices will be higher than in the Mercado Modelo, but the quality will be better.

Mercado Modelo Turístico, Calle del Sol and Av España, Santiago. *Outside town, on Autopista Duarte.* Many potteries where ceramics are cheap.

In Puerto Plata, the **Mercado Viejo**, Ureña and Separación. Sells mostly hardware and furniture, although there is also a *botánica* which sells items relating to syncretist religion, witchcraft, voodoo and folk healing. The **Mercado Nuevo**, at Isabela de Torres and Villanueva, sells handicrafts, rum, Cuban cigars, Haitian art and other souvenirs.

Mercado Artesanal, Bibijagua, Bávaro. *Just along the beach from the Barceló complex.* Bibijagua, cleverly signed as BI.JH.O, is a large covered market on the beach where you can buy handicrafts, rum, cigars (likely to be fakes), T-shirts, paintings (copies of Haitian art) and other souvenirs, but don't buy the shells, turtles and stuffed sharks which are for sale, as they are protected by international treaties and should be impounded by customs officials on your return home.

Museo del Hombre Dominicano, Plaza de la Cultura, Santo Domingo, **T** 6894672. *Tue-Sun 1000-1700. Map 2, D4, p253.* Gift shop sells ceramics, Taíno reproductions and works of anthropological interest. See also page 49.

Jewellery

Museo Mundo de Ambar, Arzobispo Meriño 452, esq Restauración, Santo Domingo, **T** 6823309. *Mon-Sat 0800-1800, Sun 0800-1300. Map 1, B4, p252.* Museum, workshop and shop, see page 43.

Museo del Ambar, Duarte 61 esq Emilio Prud'homme, Puerto Plata, **T** 5862848, www.ambermuseum.com. *Mon-Sat 0900-1800.* Museum and gift shop, see page 67. Amber Museum Shop also at Playa Dorada Plaza, **T** 3202215, and at Marien Coral by Hilton, Costa Dorada, **T** 3201515. *Daily 0800-2200.*

Museo de Ambar, El Conde 107 on Parque Colón, Santo Domingo, **T** 6864471. *Map 1, D5, p252.* Small museum upstairs, with a shop on the ground floor selling amber, larimar, protected black coral (don't buy it), local gold and pearls.

Museo de Larimar , Isabel La Católica, Santo Domingo, **T** 6896605. *Mon-Fri 0830-1800, Sun 0900-1300. Free. Map 1, E5, p252*

Museum and shop with examples of this lovely pale blue stone found only in the Dominican Republic.

Music

The best place in Santo Domingo to get all kinds of music is **Musicalia Outlet**, El Conde, Zona Colonial, **T** 2218445, another shop at Tiradentes esq Gustavo Mejía Ricart, **T** 5622878. Other music shops include: **CD Mania**, Av Venezuela 104, **T** 5915698; **CD Stop**, Plaza Central, **T** 5495640; **Music Box**, Los Jardines, Arroyo Hondo, **T** 5403055; **Karen Records**, El Conde 251, Zona Colonial, **T** 6860019; and **Tiagos**, El Conde, Zona Colonial, **T** 6896154.

Shopping malls

In Santo Domingo there are some 20 shopping malls, including **Plaza Naco**, Av Tiradentes y Naco, **Unicentro Plaza**, Av 27 de Febrero esq Av Abraham Lincoln, **Plaza Caribe**, Av 27 de Febrero esq Leopoldo Navarro, **Multicentro Churchill**, Av Winston Churchill esq Gustavo Mejía Ricart, **Acropolios Mall** on Av Winston Churchill entre Roberto Pastoriza y Gustavo Mejía Ricart, **Bella Vista Mall**, Sarasota entre Dr Defiló y Winston Churchill, **Diamond Mall**, Los Próceres, Arroyo Hondo, all offering a variety of shops, food halls, restaurants, cinemas, banks and offices.

Playa Dorada Plaza, or **Centro Comercial**, is the first real shopping mall on the north coast. Prices are slightly inflated, but the quality of all items, especially the locally-made ceramics, jewellery, and clothing, is superior to most sold by beach or street vendors. The mall includes a Bennetton, a selection of Tiffany lamps and some very original jewellery. Cigars, leather goods, amber, larimar, coffee and rum can all be found here.

Sport is an integral part of Dominican life, with baseball being the number one spectator sport and every small boy dreaming of becoming a star. In addition to the many players in the US baseball leagues, the Dominican Republic has produced athletes of great renown in other sports, such as the Olympic champion hurdler, Félix Sánchez, and the up-and-coming high jumper, Juana Arrendell, who won gold in the 2003 Pan-American Games, held in Santo Domingo. For the occasion, the Government invested heavily in world-class sports facilities, most of which are in the Parque Mirador del Este. A team of 40 athletes travelled to the 2004 Olympic Games in Athens, competing in sports such as boxing, judo, weightlifting, table tennis, volleyball and track and field.

The visitor to the country is more likely to be interested in the many watersports, adventure sports or golf in which he or she can participate. Windsurfing and kiteboarding are big in Cabarete, while the mountains around Jarabacoa offer challenging river sports and hiking.

The manicured greens of immaculate golf courses dot the coastline, offering hours of entertainment, while the more energetic can get off the beaten track with a mountain bike to cycle through the countryside. Scuba diving is varied and many large pelagic fish can be seen around the island, while snorkelling is also rewarding.

Baseball

The national sport is baseball. The Dominican Republic has produced a phenomenal number of great players and the game has become known as a way out of poverty, with thousands of boys hoping to be plucked out of obscurity by team selectors and paid a fortune to play their favourite game. The best players are recruited by US and Canadian teams who maintain feeder academies in the Republic; about half of the 500 professional Dominican players in the USA come from San Pedro de Macorís. The regular season starts on the last Friday in October and runs until the end of December, with national and big league players participating. For three weeks at the beginning of January, round robin semi-final matches are held, after which the two best teams compete in the Serie Final in the last week of January.

Basketball

Basketball is the second most popular sport, played on an amateur basis in the Olympic centre, the Palacio de los Deportes and in sports clubs around the country. There are also matches at the Club San Lázaro and Club San Carlos. Every town has a good outdoor court where they play every evening and anyone can join in. The talent is good, there are a lot of Dominicans in the NBA. Be careful of slippery courts and keep your elbows out!

Bowling

Sebelén Bowling Centre (Bolera), Av Abraham Lincoln, esq Roberto Pastoriza, Santo Domingo, **T** 5400101. *1000-0200.*

Map 2, D2, p253 Bowling has now become a hugely popular pastime. This centre, built to host the 1997 Pan-American Bowling Games, is said to be the world's most hi-tech bowling alley.

Boxing

Boxing matches take place frequently in Santo Domingo at the Gimnasio-Coliseo de Boxeo (with a capacity to seat 7,000 but capable of holding 10,000 spectators) next to the baseball stadium. They can also be seen at the Carlos Teo Cruz Coliseum, at hotels and at sports clubs, where you can also see fencing, judo, karate and table tennis.

Cockfighting

Coliseo Gallístico de Santo Domingo, Av Luperón, near Herrera Airport, Santo Domingo, **T** 5653844. *Map 3, F7, p255* Fights are on Saturday and Sunday, tickets from US$2, but the spectacle can equally well be seen at any rural town or village. Sunday is the big day for cockfighting, although you will often see them practising on other days. A fighting cock is a treasured bird, well-groomed and lovingly cared for by his owner. He will be carried upright, balanced in the crook of a man's arm, whereas his unfortunate female companion will be held upside down.

Cycling

The Dominican Republic has miles of dirt roads and endless mule trails, making it a paradise for mountain bikers. The coastal routes are breathtaking, but can change quickly after hurricanes and rain storms. The majority of cyclists visit in the winter, although June to October is the driest time when most tracks are open.

Some bike shops and hotels have bikes to rent. However, they are rarely well maintained and are usually only suitable for a coastal cruise. The two main places to rent mountain bikes are Iguana Mama and Rancho Baiguate.

Sports

Iguana Mama, Cabarete, **T** 5710908, www.iguanamama.com. The only licensed biking tour operator on the north coast. Offers guided daily mountain biking as well as several multi-day tours covering the whole country, including 9-day Dominican Alps and 12-day Coast to Coast.

Rancho Baiguate, Jarabacoa, **T** 5746890, www.ranchobaiguate.com.do. The largest adventure sports centre in the mountains, offering bikes and quad bikes as well as rafting, canyoning and tubing.

Diving and snorkelling

There are relatively few underwater parks, but the tropical reef is diverse, interesting and in good condition. There are over 50 species of hard coral (the form that builds reefs) and a colourful variety of soft coral. The quantity of fish varies; some areas have depleted stocks because of spearfishing. Nevertheless, in Dominican waters you can see whales, dolphins, groupers, barracuda and other large pelagics, as well as lots of colourful reef fish, turtles and invertebrates. May to September are usually the best months, when the sea is calm and the visibility good. In high season, December to April, there can often be winds and rain which stir up the sand, reduce visibility and bring in a lot of rubbish which litters the dive sites.

In the Puerto Plata area the diving is best around Sosúa. More conservation-minded divers should head further east to Río San Juan, where there are plans to make the area offshore of the Laguna Grí Grí an underwater park. The Samaná peninsula offers rewarding diving on its north side and there are several dive shops at Las Terrenas and one at Las Galeras. There are dive sites all around the bays and headlands, such as Cabo Cabrón, and out to Cayo de las Ballenas. Bayahibe on the southeast coast offers some of the best diving in the country. There are nice dive sites all along the coast to Saona island, including La Parguera and the islands of

Catalina and Catalinita. Nearer to Santo Domingo is La Caleta underwater park.

Dive Samaná, Casa Marina Hotel, Las Galeras, **T** 8407926/3241696. Peter Traubel and his multilingual staff run CMAS courses (US$340 for the first stage). Single dive (US$38), six dives (US$195), snorkelling (US$10). The boat is small, with only limited shade.

Grí Grí Divers, Gaston Deligne 4, Río San Juan, *near the Hotel Bahía Blanca,* **T** 5892357, D.McEachron@verizon.net.do. Staff are multilingual, helpful and friendly. PADI courses offered: resort course (US$75); advanced open water (US$285); full certification (US$450). Single dive (US$45); two dives on the same day (US$70).

GUS Dive Center, Santo Domingo, **T** 5660818, gusdive@verizon.net.do. SSI certification. Possibly the best dive centre in the capital with rental gear and scheduled dive trips.

Mark Goldsmith, Santo Domingo, **T** 6977996, ddbconsultants@verizon.net.do. British, gives PADI certification, classes in English, very professional.

Mike's Dive Center, Santo Domingo, **T** 5663483, dive@verizon.net.do. A small dive shop renting scuba gear and arranging miscellaneous trips to different dive sites on demand. Dive master, Emiliano García, is very friendly and professional.

Northern Coast Aquasports/Diving, Pedro Clisante 8, Sosúa, **T** 5711028, www.northerncoastdiving.com. Multilingual staff, boats in Sosúa and at Grí Grí. Good for novice or experienced divers, probably the most professional operation on this stretch of coast. Two-tank dive (US$60); open water course (US$325);

beginner's course (US$60); snorkelling trips (US$25 for 1 ½ hrs, US$40 for 3 ½ hrs) and Grí Grí day trip with a cruise, snorkelling, lunch (US$85).

Scubafun, Calle Principal 28, Bayahibe, **T** 1-8330003, www.scubafun.info. Run by Germans Werner and Martina Marzilius. Flexible excursions. Two-tank dives with beach stop (US$55); trip to Saona or Catalina (additional US$30 or US$40 including park fees, tank, weights, drinks and snacks); PADI open water course (US$295).

Fishing

Several international fishing tournaments are held each year, the catch being blue marlin, bonito and dorado. There is an annual deep-sea fishing tournament at Boca de Yuma, east of La Romana, in June. For information about fishing contact **Santo Domingo Club Náutico**, Lope de Vega 55, **T** 5661682, or the **Clubes Náuticos** at Boca Chica, **T** 6854940, Cabeza de Toro, near Bávaro, and at Monte Cristi. However, these clubs are for members only, so you will need to know someone who is a member if you want to visit. For instruction contact **Actividades Acuáticas** at Boca Chica, **T** 5234511.

Golf

Golf is big business here, with much of the east and north coasts devoted to the sport. There are over two dozen golf courses with more being built. All the biggest and newest resorts have a golf course attached. There are also courses around Santo Domingo, Bávaro and Altos de Chavón.

Descriptions of many of the golf courses can be found on www.dr1.com/travel/special/golf.hstml and there is a helpful map on www.dominicanrepinfo.com/Golf.htm.

The Tourist Office publishes a Golf Guide, which can be ordered online, www.golfguide-do.com. The **Dominican Golf Association** organizes tournaments all year round, **T** 4764898.

Casa de Campo, **T** 5232480, **F** 5238800. *Teeth of the Dog* Green fee US$175 including cart, par 72 Championship course designed by Pete Dye. Eight of the holes are right on the sea, judged one of the most beautiful courses in the world. There are two other courses at Caso de Campo: *The Links* and *Altos de Chavón*, plus *La Romana Country Club (*members only).

Las Aromas, Santiago, **T** 2765396. Green fee US$13, par 70. Hilly, with lovely views of the Cibao valley, wide fairways and lots of trees.

Playa Dorada, near Puerto Plata, **T** 3726020, **F** 3202773, *0700-1730* Green fee US$45, including cart, extra charge for mandatory caddy, par 72 Championship course designed by Robert Trent Jones Sr as part of a complex of all-inclusive hotels outside Puerto Plata.

Playa Grande, near Río San Juan, **T** 2485313, **F** 2485314. Green fee US$81 including cart, par 72 course also designed by Robert Trent Jones Sr. Ten of its holes along the coast on top of cliffs.

Hiking

The Dominican Republic provides ideal conditions for medium-distance walking in the tropics; distances and temperatures are manageable. The Cordillera Central is home to the two highest peaks in the Caribbean: Pico Duarte (3,087 m) and La Pelona (3,082 m). Hiking up Pico Duarte is now a major attraction, see page 59 for further details. There is a fee of RD$50 to enter any national park in the Republic and you must always be accompanied by a guide.

Olympic gold for Super Sanchez

The 2004 Olympic Games in Athens saw the Dominican Republic bring home its first gold medal in over 20 years. Felix 'Super' Sanchez won the 400-metre hurdles in a stunning 47.63 seconds, easily beating his competitors. Prior to the Olympics, he won gold at the Pan American Games in Santo Domingo in 2003 and was unbeaten in over 40 outings. The only other gold medal that the country has seen was in the 1984 Games in Los Angeles when boxer, Pedro Julio Nolasco, became the first Dominican ever to bring home the gold.

Other areas for rewarding hiking are around Jarabacoa, Constanza and in the Valle Nuevo National Park, while easy climbs can be done up Pico Yaque, Mount Isabel de Torres outside Puerto Plata, or in the Sierra de Baoruco in the southwest.

Iguana Mama, Cabarete, **T** 5710908, www.iguanamama.com. Offers tours for individuals and groups to national parks on the north coast and to Pico Duarte.

Rancho Baiguate, Jarabacoa, **T** 5746890, www.ranchobaiguate.com.do. Can arrange hikes to Pico Duarte and other walks in the Cordillera Central.

Tours Trips Treks & Travel, Cabarete, **T** 8678884, www.4tdomrep.com. Organizes customized expeditions for small or large groups to all national parks, focussing on anthropology, history, geography and community service.

Sports

Horse racing

Horse racing takes place at the **Hipódromo V Centenario** at Km 14.5 on the Autopista de las Américas, **T** 6876060, grandstand ticket US$1.

Polo matches are played at weekends at Sierra Prieta, 25 minutes from Santo Domingo, and at Casa de Campo (see below).

Horse riding

Riding is available in several places but the mountains descending to the north coast are especially rewarding. Be particular when going on a horse and check that it is well looked after with no sores or lameness. No one wears a hard hat, so check your insurance policy before setting out along mountain trails.

Casa de Campo, outside La Romana, **T** 5233333. The very best horses are kept here, including polo ponies and showjumpers. Offers specialist tuition in most disciplines.

Rancho Al Norte, Jamao, on the north coast, **T** 2230660, www.unclebobsranch.com. Offers horse riding and tubing with refreshments, light meals and transport, US$75.

Rancho Montana, on the north coast, one hour east of Puerto Plata, **T** 2485407, www.ranchomontana.com. Takes you riding along dry river beds and through mountains with snacks, drinks and transport, US$65.

Kiteboarding

Kiteboarding is the newest and most exciting watersport around the world, and Cabarete is considered by those who know to be the best location for the sport. The western end of Cabarete beach, known as Kite Beach, is used for kiteboarding, away from the windsurfers. In the summer, the sea is flat calm, with winds

Sports

side-onshore, picking up around 1100-1300, making the mornings good for training. The Kiteboarding World Cup is held here annually in June, with top international kiteboarders competing. Four Dominicans are among the top 32 kiteboarders in the world. For information see www.cabaretekiteboarding.com.

Cabarete Kiteboarding Center, Kitebeach Hotel, **T** 5710878, www.kiteworldcabarete.com. Equipment rental and storage, teaching in Spanish, Italian and English.

Caracol Kiteboarding Centre, by Laurel Eastman, Caracol Beach Club, **T** 5710564, www.caracolkiteboarding.com. Offers good equipment and lessons at all levels, including women-only clinics, massage, kite-cleaning facilities, storage and sales.

Dare2Fly, Kitebeach, **T** 5710805, www.dare2fly.com. Good school, part of an international chain, offering courses for beginners and equipment rental for all levels. The centre has many facilities: a bar/restaurant, lockers, parking and restrooms.

Kitexcite, Kitexcite Hotel, **T** 5719509, www.kitexcite.com. Private lessons are US$300 for three days, less for more people. After that you can rent equipment, US$45-60 a day, weekly rates available for kites and boards.

Paragliding/parapenting

Simon Vacher, Jarabacoa, off the road to Rancho Baiguate, **T** 8821201, simonvacher@yahoo.com. Tandem flights, parapenting and paragliding.

River sports

Jarabacoa is the centre for watersports, being blessed with three main rivers, the Río Yaque del Norte, the Jimenoa and the

Baiguate, and their many tributaries. Whitewater rafting, canyoning, tubing and kayaking are all on offer. The rainy season is more exciting than the dry season because the more water there is the faster it flows. Information can be found at www.DRpure.com, www.hispaniola.com/whitewater and www.ranchobaiguate.com.do.

Aventuras del Caribe, Ranch Jarabacoa, **T/F** 5742669, franz.lang@verizon.net.do.   Run by Franz Lang, an Austrian. He deals with small groups, is recommended for canyoning and kayaking and is very safety conscious.

Máxima Aventura, Rancho Baiguate, **T** 5746890, www.ranchobaiguate.com.do.   The biggest adventure sports centre with a small army of Dominican and international specialist guides and instructors for each activity. They also own **Get Wet**, **T** 5861170, which offers the same river activities.

Sailing
For renting boats and yachts, contact the Secretaría de Turismo (see page 33). There are no charter fleets at present. The Punta Cana Resort has a brand new marina and so does Casa de Campo, www.casadecampomarina.com. Most beach resorts have small craft for rent by the hour or the half day. For independent yachtsmen the Dominican Republic is an excellent place to reprovision if cruising the islands.

Surfing
Guibia is a great surfing beach near Santo Domingo, but it is full of garbage and oil from the ships going to Ozama. Other surf beaches

! In 2004 the government banned the use of jet skis off most beaches. There are a few exceptions in areas that are away from swimmers.

include Baoruco and Playa Pato in Barahona, La Preciosa, La Pasa and Playa Grande in Río San Juan, El Encuentro (with a consistent break off the left and right) and El Canal in Cabarete, Sosúa bay and La Boca in Sosúa, La Puntilla in Puerto Plata, Cofresí west of Puerto Plata, and El Macao near Bávaro in the east.

Del Mar, El Encuentro Beach, Cabarete, **T** 3602576, www.delmarcabarete.com.   Surf boards cost US$15 for a half day. Very friendly, multilingual instructors. The Surf Café has welcome refreshments as well as barbecue.

No Work Team, El Encuentro Beach, Cabarete, **T** 5710820.   Offers daily minisurf course, board rentals, boogie board rentals and surf camps. They also issue a wind and wave report, updated twice a week for the Cabarete area. There is an excellent shop for sports clothing and beach wear.

Surf & Sport surfing school, Cabarete, **T** 5710463.   Run by long-time local surfer, Markus Bohm, offers daily lessons, US$25, for all ages and levels.

Windsurfing
Cabarete, near Sosúa, is one of the best windsurfing places in the world, attracting international competitors to tournaments. Cabarete is the place to be in June, when the town is taken over by serious windsurfers for Cabarete Race Week. See www.cabaretewindsurfing.com or www.cabareteevents.com for further information.

The winds are at their best for Race Week, but windsurfing takes place all year round. In summer (mid-June to mid-September) there are constant trade winds but few waves. In winter there is less wind, but the waves can be tremendous. The mornings are generally calm, with the wind picking up in the afternoon. The windsurfing schools are all good, with excellent equipment.

Boards rent for around US$50 per day, US$200 per week; make sure insurance is available. Schools offer multilingual lessons. Most of them stock other watersports equipment, too, such as surf boards and kayaks.

Carib Bic Center, Cabarete, **T** 5710640, www.caribwind.com. Excellent windsurfing gear for rent, with professional and experienced instructors, and the best surf shop in town. They have a full watersports centre with sea kayaks, boogie boards, surfboards, hobie cats and snorkelling gear.

Club Mistral, Pequeño Refugio Hotel, Cabarete, **T** 5719791, www.cabaretewindsurfing.com/mistral. Part of an international company with a team of qualified instructors. Caters for beginners to advanced and wave freaks. Kayaks and kiteboarding also available.

Club Nathalie Simon, Cabarete, **T** 5710848. French speaking. Tuition for all levels, including children from five years old who can start on the lagoon behind the beach.

Fanatic, Cabarete, **T** 5710861, www.fanatic-cabarete.com. German speaking. Offers equipment rental and courses for adults. They also offer babysitting services for while you are out on the water.

Vela, Cabarete, **T** 5710805, www.velawindsurf.com. Reliable. Equipped with the latest in high-performance gear, styled boards available for rent. Beginner courses and free windsurf clinics. Integrated with Dare2fly kiteboarding school.

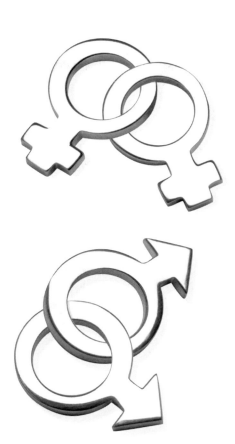

While the environment for open homosexuality in the Dominican Republic has changed significantly over the past five years and the re-election of Leonel Fernández and the PLD party in May 2004 is expected to bring another wave of more liberal transformations, it still does not enjoy many of the accepted and established means of gay and lesbian travel that some other islands of the Caribbean do. The Dominican Republic is still far from an environment where anything goes, but many pockets exist where you can be free.

In a patriarchal country where 95% of the population is stated Roman Catholic and more than 15% are illiterate, traditional and conservative lifestyles and ways of thinking are held dear. There are no explicit laws against homosexuality in the Dominican Republic, yet the police have historically used the tenets of 'public disturbance' as a cover. There are no openly gay clubs, with perhaps the exception of Aire in the Zona Colonial of Santo Domingo.

There was a brief exception to this during the 500th anniversary of the European Encounter in 1992. With the renovations and investments in the Zona Colonial for the celebration, homosexuals experienced a period of 'open time' where several bars and clubs were openly gay and lesbian. By 1994 however, police officials were already cracking down and closing establishments predominantly for use of illicit drugs and 'public disturbances'.

The lesbian movement is growing, particularly in Santo Domingo, and is much stronger than that of gay men. There is a greater sense of unity among women, whereas men have been unable to present a unified front for their sexuality. The Dominican Republic is undoubtedly a macho society where men rule the roost outside the home and feel the need to express their machismo through *piropos*, or cat calls or unsolicited comments, to women passing by. They are threatened by gay men's redefinition of masculinity and have, at times, reacted through public harassment. Entrenched within Dominican Spanish are put-downs and condescending terms, like *maricón* and *condango*, that translate to slang references of gay men.

Yet not to despair, there are still many places for all walks of life in the Dominican Republic where you can be yourself, albeit not completely in the open, and more are opening every year. With improved standards of living in larger cities, increased foreign investment and a growing middle class with North American and European tastes, gays and lesbians are finding themselves in an environment of increasing tolerance, rather than acceptance. Change is predominantly driven by the youth of the middle class who do not have access to some of the upper-class freedoms and are no longer willing to go to the marginalized, and more 'dangerous', neighbourhoods to be themselves. The very rich and the very poor have, in a very general way, had an easier time of expressing their homosexuality. The middle class's process of self discovery is bringing about a slow, but assured, wave of social change.

Foreigners are rarely judged nor expected to conform to the same standards as native Dominicans and tend to draw less attention in Santo Domingo as it is the capital. The historic and picturesque Zona Colonial is probably the only place in Santo Domingo where a man can kiss a man in a bar and not be thrown out. The scenes can generally be divided between bars, clubs and pick-up-and-pay locals. Santiago, the second city of the country, has nightlife somewhat comparable to that of the Zona Colonial, albeit a bit harder to find. The north coast with its constant flux of international tourists tends to be a bit more laid-back in terms of acceptance and dress. The beach and sport town of Cabarete is the most cosmopolitan and friendly place in the country where just about anything goes in terms of display, with the exception of drugs, in all bars and restaurants. The beach bars of Las Terrenas on the northern side of the Samaná peninsula are a bit more expensive and a lot more romantic. Barring a rave or other nationally organized party, it is more a place to take that special someone for a getaway rather than pick him or her up. Outwardly gay and lesbian individuals who want to flaunt it are probably best advised to stick to the more touristy places and avoid the clubs and bars off the beach area.

Sleeping

D-E Club Escape Caribe, Hotel Playa Laguna, Playa Escondido, Cabarete, **T** 5713560, www.clubescapecaribe.com. Owned by Americans, Arthur and Kari, Club Escape Caribe is a boutique hotel serving gay and lesbian travellers in Cabarete and Sosúa. Currently based in the German-owned Playa Laguna Hotel on the main road between Sosúa and Cabarete. All rooms have fan, a/c, small refrigerator, private bath with hot water, vaulted ceilings, and an interesting colonial-Caribbean style. The hotel is quiet with bar, restaurant, small spa, and access to a beach only a 5-minute walk from the front door. Club Escape is constantly looking for new properties, so check the website to see where the newest facility is and make reservations.

Bars

Bar Phoenix, Polvorín 10, Zona Colonial, Santo Domingo, **T** 6897572. *Map 1, E0, p252* Neighbourhood bar, gay-friendly, British-run.

El Callao, in the carnavalesque-area of the Monument, Santiago. This is the oldest gay bar in Santiago. Having no walls, everyone seems to be on display. This bar has never been closed down as there is no place to hide any activity suspicious to authorities and conservatives.

Me Voy Corriendo, 27 de Febrero, Santiago. A lesbian hang-out favoured by the younger crowd. It is more of a *colmado* or *bodega* as its bar is very tiny. Without the stigma of a gay bar, patrons tend to sit on chairs on the sidewalk relaxing, talking, and enjoying a few drinks watching the city pass by.

Tailú Bar & Grill, Sabana Larga 166, Santiago, **T** 5820233. Like El Callao, close to the Monument, gay-friendly and gay-frequented, is a bit more discreet and upmarket. It is big on Fridays as the starter bar of the night.

Clubs

When attending a club, universal precautions apply: stay away from minors, keep your personal belongings safe, make sure that somebody knows who you left with, and if you are visiting a pick-up-and-pay venue, establish ahead of time if money will be expected.

A-Club, Arzobispo Nouel entre Hostos y Duarte, Santo Domingo. *From 2100. Map 1, E4, p252* Shows on selected nights frequented by *bugarones* or *sankipankies* with the pick-up-and-pay mentality. No cover charge.

Aire, Calle Mercedes 313, Santo Domingo, **T** 6894163, www.arenadisco.com. *Wed-Sun 2200-late. Map 1, D2, p252* US$3 depending on the night. Part of an international chain of clubs in colonial house with large patio and open garden area. The DJs are excellent, spinning house and dance music until the early morning hours. There is a Foam Party on Wednesdays; drag and stripper shows on Sundays; and on Saturdays there is a Message Party where guests can send messages to one another through the DJ booth.

Atlantis Disco, Av George Washington 555, Zona Colonial, Santo Domingo, **T** 6852011, www.atlantis-disco.com. *Thu-Sun, from 2300. Map 2, E4, p253* Different gay shows every night with male strippers, transvestites and drag queens. Large dance floor, two bars.

Llegó, José Reyes 10 esq Arzobispo Nouel, Zona Colonial, Santo Domingo, **T** 6898250. *From 2100. Map 1, E3, p252* No cover charge. Also frequented by *bugarones* or *sankipankies* with the pick-up-and-pay mentality. Piano bar with videos and male strippers.

Kids of all ages will love the beaches of the Dominican Republic, which are probably the main reason for any family to visit the country. Miles of golden sand and calm blue waters provide endless choice for a beach holiday. Cabarete is the in-place for windsurfing and kiteboarding entertainment; windsurfing can be taught from the age of five so the whole family can join in. The sandcastle competition in February is also a delight for the little ones. Elsewhere, glass-bottom boat tours and learning to snorkel will encourage discovery of the creatures of the sea, while whale watching in Samaná from January to March is a thrill they'll never forget. Adventure and entertainment can be found inland as well: they can get close to nature in a tropical setting in the mountains, or in the rolling hills of cattle ranches and banana plantations. Older children can engage in river rafting or hiking, while small ones can be taken on a bike ride through the fields and villages to see the rural environment. Larger hotels usually have a selection of indoor activities and games for a rainy day.

Eating and drinking

Kids are accepted everywhere and Dominican restaurants are very child-friendly. Buffet restaurants in hotels are good for even the pickiest eaters and there are plenty of American fast food restaurants, pizza places, and local fried chicken eateries. Pasta is popular and can be found in most restaurants. Beach bars usually do burgers and a variety of other options. Things become even easier if your child likes fish. Roadside stalls sell fresh fruit in season; bananas are easy to eat on the go, but mangoes should perhaps be reserved for the bath. Hotels and bars use drinking water to make ice, but avoid iced drinks sold on the street as these can cause stomach upsets. A wide range of fizzy bottled drinks is available as well as fruit juices in cartons if you can't get the fresh variety.

Attractions

★ **Mount Isabel de Torres**, 1 km past Puerto Plata. *Entrance south of the Circunvalación del Sur on a paved road marked* teleférico. *Daiy except Wed 0830-1700. US$5. Map 3, A4, p254. See also p68.* A cable car to the summit of Loma Isabel de Torres is an exciting experience for children. The view is impressive, and there are craft shops, a restaurant and botanical gardens.

Museo del Ambar, Duarte 61 esq Emilio Prud'homme, Puerto Plata, **T** 5862848, www.ambermuseum.com. *Mon-Sat 0900-1800. US$1.50.* Children will enjoy looking for insects in the resin, particularly if they've seen Jurassic Park, and learning how to test whether amber is real or fake. See also page 67.

Reserva Antropológica de las Cuevas de las Maravillas
Cumayasa,15 km from San Pedro. **T** 6961797. *Tue-Sun 1000-1800.*

Kids

Kids stuff

Some hotels have their own water purification system, but it is safer only to give bottled water to children, and plenty of it, to prevent dehydration and consequent tummy upsets. Avoid sunburn with frequent applications of a high-factor waterproof sun cream and try and keep children out of the sun completely between 1100 and 1500. Remember that the wind burns and even on a cloudy day they can catch the sun. Boat trips are a particular hazard in the battle for skin care. Babysitters are readily available and cheap. Ask your hotel for their recommendations.

Adults US$2, children under 12 US$1. Map 3, F10, p255 See also p83
Huge caves with easy access for children. Museum, shop, cafeteria and toilets.

Salto Baiguate 4 km from Jarabacoa. *Map 3, C5, p254 See also p57*
Waterfalls with a sandy river beach, safe for bathing.

Salto de Limón 10 km southeast of Las Terrenas. *Map 3, C9, p255 See also p80* Older children can ride to the waterfall which has a safe pool for swimming.

Whale Samaná, Victoria Marine, Samaná, **T** 5382494, www.whalesamana.com. *Jan-Mar 0900 and 1330, US$45.*
A fascinating whale-watching tour for children, with careful explanations in several languages. They also dish out sea-sickness pills beforehand. See also page 77.

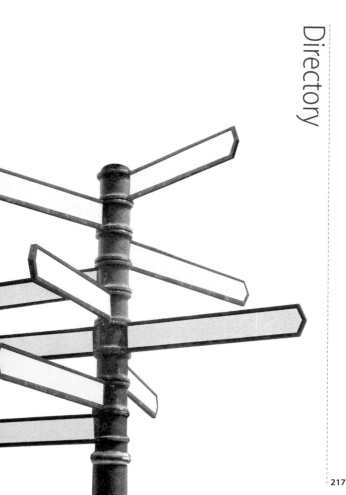

217

Airline offices

Air Europa, Av Winston Churchill 459, Santo Domingo, **T** 6838020. **Air France**, Av Máximo Gómez 15, Santo Domingo, **T** 6868432; at Las Américas International Airport, **T** 5490309; at Punta Cana Airport, **T** 9593002. **Air Jamaica**, F P Ramírez 159, Santo Domingo, **T** 8720080. **Air Santo Domingo**, Av 27 de Febrero 272 esq Seminario, Santo Domingo, **T** 6838006, information and reservations, **T** 6838020; at Herrera Airport **T** 6836691; at Las Américas **T** 5491110; at La Romana Airport, **T** 8139144; at Puerto Plata Airport, **T** 5860391; at Punta Cana **T** 2211170/9592473; at Puerto Plata **T** 5860385; at El Portillo, Samaná, **T** 2406571. **American Airlines**, Edif In Tempo, Av Winston Churchill, Santo Domingo, **T** 5425151; La Romana Airport, **T** 5565786; Punta Cana Airport, **T** 9597002. **American Eagle**, Las Américas, Santo Domingo, **T** 5492339; Puerto Plata Airport, **T** 5860325. **Caribair**, caribair.sa@verizon.net.do, Av Luperón, Santo Domingo, **T** 5426688; La Romana, **T** 2218076; Puerto Plata, **T** 6829855; Punta Cana, **T** 6885542. **Condor**, Av George Washington 353, Santo Domingo, **T** 6853125. **Continental**, Av Winston Churchill, Santo Domingo, **T** 5626688. **Copa**, 27 de Febrero, Santo Domingo, **T** 4722233. **Coturisca**, Av Luperón 49, Santo Domingo, **T** 6833435. **Cubana**, Av Tiradentes, Santo Domingo, **T** 2272040, ventascuba@verizon.net.do. **Iberia**, Lope de Vega 63, Santo Domingo, **T** 5080188. **Lufthansa**, Av George Washington 353, Santo Domingo, **T** 6899625. **Martinair**, Maximo Gómez y Juan S Ramírez, Santo Domingo, **T** 6886661. **Mexicana de Aviación**, Av G M Ricart 54, Santo Domingo, **T** 5411016. **Sky King**, Puerto Plata International Airport, **T** 5860342. **United Airlines**, G M Ricart 54, Santo Domingo, **T** 5418072. **US Airways**, G M Ricart 54, Santo Domingo, **T** 5400505.

Banks and ATMs

Scotiabank (Santo Domingo and other cities), **Banco León** (Santo Domingo and other cities), **Citibank** (Santo Domingo and

Santiago), **BanReservas** (Santo Domingo and other cities), **Banco Popular**, **Banco Mercantil**, **Banco Central**, **Banco del Progreso**, **Banco BHD** and others. Money can be sent via Western Union, which operates through Vimenca but the exchange rate is up to 20% more than banks. Most banks have 24-hour ATMs outside or in the lobby. ATH (A Toda Hora) allows you to make purchases in shops with the ATH and Maestro logo and you can obtain cash 24 hours a day through any ATM connected to ATH with a Mastercard, Cirrus, Visa or Plus logo.

Bicycle hire

Iguana Mama, Cabarete, **T** 5710908, www.iguanamama.com.
Rancho Baiguate, Jarabacoa, **T** 5746890,
www.ranchobaiguate.com.do.

Car hire

MC Auto Rent-A-Car, Av George Washington 105, Santo Domingo, **T** 6886518, **F** 6864529, www.mccarrental.com, branches also at Las Américas Airport, **T** 5498911 and Boca Chica, **T** 5234414. **Nelly**, Av Independencia 654, Santo Domingo, **T** 6877979; Playa Dorada, **T** 3204888; at Puerto Plata Airport, **T** 5860505, from US$45 a day. **Dollar**, Av Independencia, Santo Domingo, **T** 2217368, from US$47 a day. **Hertz**, Av Independencia 454, Santo Domingo, **T** 2215333. **Payless**, Gustavo Mejía Ricart 826, Santo Domingo, **T** 5634686. **Avis**, Gregorio Luperón International Airport, Puerto Plata, **T** 5860496. **Honda**, Carrera Luperón 2½ km, Puerto Plata, **T** 5863136; at the airport, **T** 5860233. **Puerto Plata Rent-A-Car**, Beller 7, Puerto Plata, **T** 5863141.

Credit card lines

Mastercard T 1-800-3077309, **Visa T** 800-VISA-911, for other credit cards without a local contact number, make sure you bring details from home for a number to call if your card is lost or stolen.

Disabled

Very few hotels have facilities for the disabled, although access for wheelchairs is gradually becoming more common. In Santo Domingo the best place to stay is at the Courtyard by Marriott (see page 112). Getting to the beach is tricky in a wheelchair and town pavements are potholed and often too narrow. The Wyndham Dominicus Beach Hotel in Bayahibe also caters for disabled people (see page 131).

Electricity

Voltage 110 volts, 60 cycles AC current. American-type, flat-pin plugs are used. There are frequent power cuts, often for several hours, so take a torch with you when you go out at night. Many establishments have their own (often noisy) generators.

Embassies and consulates

Austria, Las Amapolas 9, Ens Bella Vista, Santo Domingo, **T** 5080709; **Belgium**, Torre Panamericana, Piso 10, Av Abraham Lincoln 504, Santo Domingo, **T** 5442200; **Canada**, Capitán Eugenio de Marchena 39, Ens La Esperilla, Santo Domingo, **T** 6851136, sdmgo@dfait-maeci.ge.ca; **Denmark**, Torre Panamericana, Piso 10, Av Abraham Lincoln 504, Santo Domingo, **T** 5495100; **France**, Las Damas 42, Zona Colonial, Santo Domingo, **T** 6875621, ambafrance.sd@verizon.net.do; **Germany**, Rafael A Sánchez 33 esq Lope de Vega, Plaza Intercaribe, Ensanche Naco, Santo Domingo, **T** 5658811; **Haiti**, Juan Sánchez Ramírez 33, Zona Universitaria, Santo Domingo, **T** 4127112-5, amb.haiti @verizon.net.do; **Holland**, Max Henríquez Ureña 50 esq Abraham Lincoln, Ens Piantini, Santo Domingo, **T** 5653262; **Israel**, P H Ureña 80, Santo Domingo, **T** 4720776; **Italy**, Manuel Rodríguez Objío 4, Gazcue, Santo Domingo, **T** 6820830, ambital@verizon.net.do; **Spain**, Independencia 1205, Santo Domingo, **T** 5356500; **UK**, Av 27 de Febrero 233, Edificio Corominas Pepín, 7th floor, **T** 4727111, brit.emb.sadom@verizon.net.do; **USA** César Nicolás Penson esq

Leopoldo Navarro, Santo Domingo (embassy) **T** 2212171,
(consulate) **T** 2215511, webmaster.usemb.gov.do.

Emergency numbers
Ambulance, Fire and Police **T** 911.

Hospitals and medical services
Clínica Abréu, Av Independencia y Beller 42, Santo Domingo,
T 6884411, and adjacent **Clínica Gómez Patiño** are
recommended for foreigners needing treatment or hospitalization.
Fees are high but care is good. 24-hour emergency department.
For free consultation and prescription, **Padre Billini Hospital**,
Calle Padre Billini y Santomé, Zona Colonial, Santo Domingo,
efficient, friendly. **Hospital Ricardo Limardo**, J E Kunhardt,
Puerto Plata, **T** 5862210/5862237. **Servimed**, Cabarete, Main St,
by Harrison's Jewellers, **T** 5710964, medical centre, laboratory
service and dentist, open 24 hours.

Internet/email
Verizon (formerly Codetel), offices in most towns have a computer,
but can be unreliable. **Tricom** has internet access at Las Américas
Airport and a few centres in Santo Domingo. **Cybercafés** have
opened in tourist areas such as Cabarete, Boca Chica, Bayahibe and
Las Terrenas, but service is often down. In Santo Domingo,
Centennial Dominicana offices allow you to use their internet for
free. Offices at Winston Churchill esq Gustavo Mejía Ricart (Edificio
Grouconsa), Máximo Gómez esq Av Bolívar (Plaza de los
Libertadores), and Carretera Mella Km 8.5 next to the Ferretería
Haché, open Mon-Sat 0800-1900. In the Zona Colonial, **Abel
Brown's Internet World**, El Conde 359, **T** 3335604, open Mon-Sat
0900-2100, Sun 1000-1600. In Puerto Plata, **Comp.Net**, Calle 12 de
Julio 77, **T** 5864104, US$3 per hour. In Cabarete, **Telecabarete**,
T/F 5710975, open 0900-0400, US$0.04 per minute.

Language schools

The official language is Spanish, although English, German, French and Italian are spoken in tourist resorts by guides and some hotel employees. English is the language most commonly taught to tourism workers. If you are planning to travel off the beaten track, a working knowledge of Spanish is essential. **Escuela de Idiomas de la Universidad APEC**, Avenida Máximo Gómez 72, Apdo Postal 59-2, Santo Domingo, **T** 6873181, offers Spanish courses, one to two hours daily, Monday to Friday, for a term. **Instituto Cultural Domínico Americano**, Av Abraham Lincoln esq Correa y Cidrón, **T** 5350665, Spanish courses for children and adults. **Boston Institute**, Edificio La Nave, John F Kennedy, **T** 5631050.

Libraries

Biblioteca Nacional, in the Plaza de la Cultura, Santo Domingo, has a fine collection and is a good place for a quiet read. **Biblioteca República Dominicana**, Dr Delgado esq Francia, Santo Domingo, **T** 6862800, contains the Museo del Libro, with an exhibition of all the best works by Dominican authors. **Instituto Cultural Domínico Americano**, Av Abraham Lincoln esq Antonio de la Maza, Santo Domingo, English and Spanish books. The **National Congress** has a good library, as do some of the universities: **Pontífica Universidad Católica Madre y Maestra**, the **Instituto Tecnológico de Santo Domingo** and the **Universidad Autónoma de Santo Domingo**.

Media

There are six daily newspapers, four in the morning, two in the afternoon. *Listín Diario* (www.listin.com.do) has the widest circulation; among the other morning papers are *El Caribe* (www.elcaribe.com.do), *Hoy* (www.hoy.com.do), *Diario Libre* (www.diariolibre.com.do). In the afternoon, *Ultima Hora* (www.ultimahora.com.do) and *El Nacional* (www.elnacional.com.do) are published. *Primicias* is a Sunday paper. *Touring* is a multilingual tourist newspaper with articles and adverts in English, German, French, Spanish and Italian. *La Información*, published in Santiago on weekdays, is a good regional paper carrying both national and international stories. There are over 170 local radio stations and seven television stations. Cable television is available. *Cadena de Noticias* and RNN transmit news programmes 24 hours a day. *Caribbean Travelling Network* (CTN) has news of tourist sites, good for visitors.

Pharmacies (late night)
Farmacia San Judas Tadeo, Independencia 57 esq Bernardo Pichardo, Santo Domingo, **T** 6858165, open 24 hours all year, home delivery.

Police
Politur, the Tourist Police, has a toll-free phone **T** 1-200-3500, or at the office in Santo Domingo **T** 6868639. There are also **Politur** offices in Puerto Plata, Luperón, Sosúa, Cabarete, Río San Juan, Las Terrenas, Samaná, Jarabacoa, Barahona, Boca Chica, Juan Dolio, La Romana, Bávaro, and Las Américas International Airport.

Post offices
Correo Central is in La Feria, Calle Rafael Damirón, Centro de los Héroes, Santo Domingo, open Mon-Fri 0800-1600, Sat 0800-1200. **Lista de correo** (poste restante) keeps mail for two months. There are post offices in **Hotel Embajador**, **T** 2212131, **Plaza Central**, **T** 4726777, **Isabela La Católica**, Zona Colonial, **T** 6894721 and **Av George Washington**, **T** 6823439. To ensure the delivery of documents worldwide, use a courier service: **American Airlines** (**T** 5490043); **DHL Dominicana**, **T** 5437888; **Universal Courier Services**, **T** 5497398; **UPS Dominicana**, **T** 5665177; **Federal Express**, **T** 5653636; **Internacional Bonded Couriers**, **T** 5425265. Don't use post boxes, they are unreliable. The postal system as a whole is very slow. A letter to

Europe is US$0.80-US$1.50; to North America and the Caribbean, US$0.30-US$1.10; to South and Central America, Australia and Asia, US$0.50-US$1.10. You can buy postal envelopes without stamps but with pictures of tourist sites, issued by the **Instituto Postal Dominicano**. It is recommended to use *entrega especial* (special delivery, with separate window at post offices), for a little extra, on overseas mail, or better still a courier service. In Santiago the post office is at Calle del Sol esq San Luís. In Puerto Plata on 12 de Julio 42 esq Separación, **T** 5862377.

Public holidays
New Year's Day (1 Jan), Epiphany (6 Jan), Our Lady of Altagracia (21 Jan), Duarte Day (26 Jan), Independence Day (27 Feb), Good Friday (although all Semana Santa is treated as a holiday), Labour Day (1 May), Corpus Christi (60 days after Good Friday), Restoration Day (16 Aug), Our Lady of Las Mercedes (24 Sep), Christmas Day (25 Dec).

Religious services
95% of the population declares itself to be Roman Catholic, but very few people go to church on a regular basis. Saints' day festivals, *patronales*, are better attended, with the faithful turning out for the processions and parties. The **Episcopal Church**, Av Independencia 253, Santo Domingo, has services in English, from 0830 Sun. Also **Iglesia Episcopal San Andrés**, on Marcos Ruiz, Santo Domingo. The main spiritual alternative to the mainstream church is **vodú**, see box, page 185, for further details.

Taxi firms
Radio taxis charge between US$3-5 on local journeys around Santo Domingo (US$10 per hr) and are safer than street taxis, call about 20-30 mins in advance: **Taxi Anacaona**, **T** 5304800; **Apolo Taxi** (recommended), **T** 5377771; **Taxi Express**, **T** 5377777;

Taxi Oriental, **T** 5495555; **Alex Taxi**, **T** 5403311; **Taxi Hogar**, **T** 5682825; **Tecni Taxi**, **T** 5672010; **Maxi Taxi**, **T** 5440077; **Taxi Raffi**, **T** 6877858.

Telephone

The international code for the Dominican Republic is 809. Operated by **Verizon** (formerly Codetel, **T** 2201111, www.verizon.net.do), or **Tricom** (**T** 4766000 in Santo Domingo, **T** 4718000 in Santiago), call centres usually open 0800-2200. Calls and faxes may be paid for by credit card. Pre-paid calling cards are available, sold on the streets or in shops. For phone boxes you need two 1-peso coins. Call centres in the Zona Colonial: **Verizon**, El Conde 202; **Tricom**, El Conde. In Santiago, **Verizon** and **Tricom** offices are on San Luís. In Puerto Plata, **Verizon** is on Beller 48 esq Padre Castellanos; **Tricom** is at 27 de Febrero 75. Cheaper is **All American Cable & Radio** (AACR), on J F Kennedy 40.

Time

Atlantic Standard Time, four hours behind GMT, one hour ahead of Eastern Standard Time.

Tipping

In addition to the 10% service and 12% VAT charge in restaurants, it is customary in the smarter, sit-down restaurants to give an extra tip of about 10%, depending on service. Porters receive US$1-2 per bag; taxi drivers, *público* drivers and garage attendants are not usually tipped. Hotel maids appreciate tips even in all-inclusive resorts.

Toilets

Public toilets are rare, if not non-existent, and you will have to look for a hotel or bar. If you are travelling, look for roadside restaurants which offer restrooms.

Travel agents

Coco Tours, Carr Luperón, Puerto Plata, **T** 5861237, Carr Punta Cana, Higüey, **T** 6881167. **Colonial Tour & Travel**, A Meriño 209, Santo Domingo, **T** 6885285, and El Cortecito, Bávaro, Higüey, **T** 6872203, www.colonialtours.com.do. **Eco Tours**, Av B Colón 52, Santo Domingo, **T** 2474310. **Emely Tours**, Av Tiradentes, Santo Domingo, **T** 5664545, Av E Sadhalá, Santiago, **T** 7249700. **Quality Tours**, C de Moya 59, Santo Domingo, **T** 6876218. **Turinter**, LA Ginebra 24, Puerto Plata, **T** 5863911, Punta Cana, **T** 2210619, Santo Domingo, **T** 6864020, Santiago, **T** 2265342. **Viajes Vimenca**, Abraham Lincoln 310, Santo Domingo, **T** 1-200-1163.

Voluntary work

The **Dominican Republic Education and Mentoring Project** (DREAM) is based in Cabarete, **T** 8738240, www.dominicandream.org. The Executive Director is Tricia Thorndike Suriel, the founder of Iguana Mama (see page 32), and the Honorary Chairman is Julia Alvarez, the novelist (see page 237). The DREAM Project improves the education of poor children in the Dominican Republic by donating supplies, building new facilities, and placing volunteers in classrooms and libraries. Teachers and tutors are needed to work in libraries and pre-schools and provide teacher assistance in overcrowded classrooms. Children need to learn basic reading, writing and maths skills in Spanish. Doctors and nurses are also needed to give hearing and vision tests. For further information contact volunteer@dominicandream.org.

A sprint through history

1492   Recorded history of the Caribbean begins with the arrival of Christopher Columbus and his fleet on the island of Hispaniola. He tries to establish settlements, but meets with fierce resistance from the indigenous Taíno population who are consequently hunted, taxed and enslaved. The colonists squabble over land and Indian slaves as it becomes clear that there is no gold to make them wealthy.

1500   Columbus is sent home in chains. A new governor, Nicolás de Ovando, arrives and develops the capital and introduces the *encomienda* system of allocating Taíno communities to colonists as serfs.

1509   Ovando is replaced by Columbus's son, Diego. Only 60,000 Taínos remain from 400,000 in 1492. By 1524, the end of Columbus's office, practically all Taínos had been eliminated by European diseases, murder, suicide and slavery.

1551   Bartolomé de las Casas publishes *A Brief Account of the Destruction of the Indies*.

1586   Sir Francis Drake sacks Santo Domingo and the city declines in importance, overwhelmed by the onslaught of hurricanes and pirate attacks.

1697   The Treaty of Ryswick concedes the western part of the island to France which becomes the largest sugar producer in the West Indies. The Spanish colony is used for cattle ranching and supplying ships travelling from the Old World to the New.

1801-05 Following a successful slave rebellion, Haiti is proclaimed independent. The Spanish territory is

	plundered and sovereignty is disputed with frequent incursions and occupations by Haitian forces.
1822	Haiti's army takes control of Spanish Santo Domingo for 22 years, enforcing an anti-Spanish, anti-white régime. Many Spanish depart and Santo Domingo descends into poverty.
1838	The underground independence movement, *La Trinitaria*, is founded in Santo Domingo.
1844	Forces led by the writer Juan Pablo Duarte, the lawyer Francisco del Rosario Sánchez and the soldier Ramón Mella, defeat the Haitian army. The independent nation is named the Dominican Republic. Pedro Santana assumes the presidency.
1861	The Dominican Republic is re-annexed to Spain, becoming the only country in the Americas to be recolonized. Guerrillas take to the hills to fight a war of attrition, 'La Restauración', against Spain.
1865	The war is successful and Queen Isabella II abrogates the treaty of annexation and evacuates Spanish officials and troops.
1882	Ulises Heureaux takes power for a 17-year dictatorship. Germany becomes deeply involved in the economy, supporting the tobacco crop.
1905	The USA intervenes to prevent a European power gaining control of the country's customs. Roosevelt puts the Dominican customs into receivership.
1907	A formal receivership treaty is signed, heralding the start of the USA's financial leverage.

1916	The presidency collapses and US occupation begins. Dominican finances improve dramatically and the country becomes creditworthy again, but American occupiers are deeply resented. Guerrilla fighters are suppressed by US troops.
1920	The Land Registration Act is passed, allowing Dominican and US investors to purchase huge areas of land on the cheap. The dispossessed small-scale farmers form armed bands, known as *gavilleros*, and wage intermittent guerrilla warfare against the Guardia Nacional and US forces.
1924	US troops are withdrawn, but customs administration remains under US control.
1930	Presidential elections are won by the armed forces commander, Rafael Leonidas Trujillo Molina, who leads a ruthless dictatorship. He embarks on the expansion of industry and public works and the liquidation of the country's debts. However, his methods include murder, torture, blackmail and corruption.
1937	10,000 Haitian immigrants are rounded up and slaughtered, prolonging the hatred between the two republics.
1961	Trujillo is assassinated, creating another power vacuum. Violence leads to military intervention.
1962	The first free elections for 40 years are held. Joaquín Balaguer is defeated by Professor Juan Bosch of the social democratic Partido Revolucionario Dominicano (PRD), formed in exile.

1963	Bosch's policies of land reform and attacking unemployment and poverty are overwhelmingly supported by the electorate, but after just seven months a military coup sends him back into exile. Several changes of government follow.
1965	In response to civil war in the capital the USA dispatches 23,000 troops. Months of fighting ensue with the loss of some 3,000 lives.
1966	New elections are won by Balaguer, head of the Partido Reformista Social Cristiano (PRSC). US aid is crucial in rebuilding the country's economy. The US troops return home.
1970	Balaguer wins the elections and remains in office until 1978. His secret paramilitary force, *La Banda*, holds off coup attempts, right-wing terrorism and left-wing guerrilla incursions.
1978	Having boycotted previous elections, the PRD challenge Balaguer for the presidency and are successful. President Antonio Guzmán aims to reduce army power and eliminate corruption.
1982	Dr Salvador Jorge Blanco (PRD) wins the elections.
1984	Severe economic difficulties lead to rioting in which 60 people die.
1986	Balaguer (PRSC) wins a narrow majority in the elections giving him a fifth presidential term.
1990	Balaguer, accused of fraud, controversially wins a sixth term of office against Juan Bosch, now of the Partido de la Liberacion Dominicana (PLD).

1994   Balaguer is once again accused of fraud after being re-elected. His opponent, Peña Gómez (PRD) is subjected to a racist campaign of abuse because of his dark skin and alleged Haitian ancestry.

1996   Having received a majority in the first round, Peña Gómez loses the second round to Leonel Fernández (PLD) who, with Balaguer's support, wins 51% of the vote.

1997   Relations between the PRSC and the Government become strained due to land-purchase scandals involving members of the previous administration. Top ranks of the military and police are linked to drugs, unsolved murders and disappearances.

1998   Peña Gómez dies of cancer in May. Six days later, the PRD win a landslide victory in the congressional and municipal elections.

2000   Presidential elections are between 93-year-old Balaguer (PRSC), Danilo Medina (PLD) and Hipólito Mejía (PRD). Mejía wins 49.87% of the vote and is declared president after the other candidates pull out.

2002   Joaquín Balaguer dies.

2004   After a deeply unpopular presidency beset by financial scandals, economic decline, the collapse of the peso and rising inflation, Mejía loses the elections to Leonel Fernández (PLD), who takes office for a second term in August.

Sep 2004 Tropical storm Jeanne causes extensive flooding and a number of deaths.

Art and architecture

16th century	Santo Domingo was at the forefront of architectural and urban experimentation in the Spanish world. Founded by Nicolás de Ovando in 1502, the grid-plan layout set the standard for almost all subsequent Spanish foundations in the Americas. The cathedral, churches, monasteries, hospital, secular buildings both public and private, and the first fortifications along the harbour side were all solidly built of stone and brick; the styles and most of the labour were imported from Spain. The early architecture of Santo Domingo paralleled the shift in Spain from the late Gothic Isabelline style to the classicizing Plateresque but also suggested a freedom from conventional taste. Earthquakes, hurricanes and Francis Drake's attack of 1586 left a number of the early colonial buildings badly damaged and there were not the resources to restore them properly.
17th and 18th centuries	Architectural production was generally unremarkable during this time. Some country mansions and the occasional church or town hall were built, and the coastal fortifications were extended. Ambitions were modest and the means limited.
19th century	Independence in 1844 brought an increased stylistic eclecticism, especially in private housing, and some fashionable new avenues and pleasure parks. Alejandro Bonilla (1820-1901) painted the portrait of Juan Pablo Duarte in oils, and the Spaniard, José Fernández Corredor, founded the first painting school in 1883.

20th century	The dictator Trujillo initiated the building of the controversial Faro a Colón (Columbus lighthouse, see page 45). The project struggled on for 65 years, and was built at great cost amidst crushing poverty. Many considered the structure to be authoritarian and useless.
1930s	A new generation of artists came into being, including Enrique García Godoy (1886-1947) who specialized in oils and pastels, and Celeste Woss y Gil (1890-1985) who specialized in plastic arts and had a vocation for teaching and promoting women. In 1939 her oil painting *El Vendedor de Andullas* (The Tobacco Vendor) was awarded the Medal of Honor at the World Painting Exhibition in New York. The civil war in Spain brought a group of exiles to the Dominican Republic including intellectuals and artists, who helped to bring about a change in the perception and dynamics of Dominican art. Among them was José Zanetti, see box, page 49, for further information.
1940s	In 1942 a milestone was reached with the creation of the *Escuela Nacional de Bellas Artes* (National School of Fine Arts). The first graduates from this highly-respected institution in the 1940s included Marianela Jiménez, Gilberto Hernández Ortega, Domingo Liz, Ada Valcárcel, Fernando Pena de Filló and Luichi Martínez Richez, who won the Biennial Sculpture Prize in Paris in 1955.
1950s	Jaime Colson (1901-1975) emerged on the scene as the leading Dominican artist. Born in Puerto

Plata, he went on to study in Madrid and Barcelona and become one of the great painters of the American continent. His technique was refined and versatile. Colson, along with Yoryi Morel and Darío Suro, were precursors of *costumbrismo* (art of customs and manners).

1960s   Trujillo's assassination in 1961 saw an influx of foreign capital and a building boom using lots of concrete and glass. There are occasional examples of a more interesting and exotic version of Le Corbusian brutalism, as in the Cathedral of Nuestra Señora de la Altagracia in Higüey by Dunoyer de Sognzac and Pierre Dupré (see page 89). The end of Trujillo's tyranny also allowed a freedom of expression in art not permitted before.

1980 - today   The emergence of a wealthy bourgeoisie and the growth of international tourism has resulted in commissions for private houses, clubs or tourist hotels with eclectic borrowings from colonial (colonnades and porticoes), high modern (picture windows, open-plan interior spaces) and local popular architecture (wooden balconies, lattice screens), as in Placido Pina's Santo Domingo Country Club. Dominican painting has followed the themes of overcoming man's universal conflicts, such as seeking his identity, and restlessness when facing physical and ideological traumas. Those who have gained an international reputation are Iván Tovar, Ramón Oviedo, Cándido Bidó, José Rincón Mora, José Ramírez Conde and Paul Giudicelli.

Books

The US occupation of 1916-24 proved a turning point in the search for authentic forms of expression. No sooner had a radical generation of nationalist writers begun to protest against the imposition of North American values, than the long period of the Trujillo dictatorship was under way. For 30 years the régime tolerated no criticism whatsoever. Two of the 20th century's most prominent Dominican writers chose exile: the opposition leader, **Juan Bosch**, wrote polemics against Trujillo, historical studies and short stories; **Pedro Mir**, probably the greatest of the country's poets, lived and wrote abroad until the late 1960s. His works include *Hay un país en el mundo* (There's a Country in the World, 1949), and *Cuando amaban las tierras comuneras* (When They Loved the Communal Lands). The conservative **Joaquín Balaguer**, who remained on the island, wrote poetry, historical fiction and a biography of Juan Pablo Duarte. With the assassination of Trujillo in 1961, the exiles returned and politically orientated writing was again allowed. Authors such as **Manuel del Cabral** wrote incisively about the social turmoil of the 1960s in books like *La Isla ofendida* (1965), while **Freddy Prestol Castillo**'s *El Masacre se pasa a pie* (1973) was a damning account of the 1937 massacre of Haitians ordered by Trujillo.

Curiously, the dictatorship itself, although stifling literary creativity for three decades, has inspired some of the country's most interesting recent writing, notably *In the time of the Butterflies* by **Julia Alvarez** (see page 237) and *La Fiesta del Chivo* by Peruvian writer, **Mario Vargas Llosa** (see page 237) which caused unease and controversy. **Alvarez**, together with **Junot Díaz**, represents a new generation of Dominican writers, who have been as much shaped by their experience of life in the USA as in their parents' homeland, with their portrayal of alienation and cultural displacement.

Art and architecture

Nader, G, *Arte contemporáneo dominicano*. Details on contemporary Dominican painters.

Gerón, C, *Antología de la Pintura Dominicana*, *Obras Maestras de la Pintura Dominicana* (two volumes, divided into generations, or decades, of important artists) and *Pintura Dominicana, Un Cuarto de Siglo (1970-1996)*. The leading expert on all Dominican art.

Fiction

Alvarez, J, *In the Time of the Butterflies* (1994), Penguin. A fictionalized account of the events leading up to the murder by the secret police of the Mirabal sisters in 1960. *In the Name of Salomé* (2000), Penguin, is a vivid account of the politics and fear following the War of Restoration, based upon the life of the poet Salomé Ureña (1850-97). Two of her other novels, *!Yo!* (1997) and *How the García Girls Lost Their Accents* (1991), are semi-biographical and deal with exiled Dominicans growing up in the USA.

Danticat, E, *The farming of bones* (1998), The Soho Press. A powerful and emotive fictionalized account of the massacre of Haitians by Trujillo's forces in 1937, written by a Haitian now living in the USA.

Díaz, J, *Drown* (1996), Faber & Faber. A collection of short stories depicting troubled characters from the barrios of Santo Domingo to the urban Dominican communities in the USA.

Vargas Llosa, M, *La Fiesta del Chivo* (2000), *Alfaguara, The Feast of the Goat* (trans Edith Grossman), Faber & Faber. The Peruvian novelist gives a fictionalized account of the assassination of Trujillo and the intrigue and fear surrounding his period in power and the rise of Balaguer.

History

Broom, D, *Rum* (2003), Mitchell Beazley. With photographs by Jason Lowe, this beautifully illustrated book on the history of rum in the Caribbean is informative as well as entertaining.

Ferguson, J, *A Traveller's History of the Caribbean* (1998), Windrush Press. Everything the discerning traveller might want to know about the Caribbean from the Taínos to Castro.

Parry, JH, **Sherlock**, PM, **Maingot**, AP, *A Short History of the West Indies* (1987 fourth edition), Macmillan Caribbean. Putting the Dominican Republic in the context of the wider Caribbean, this history traces events from the 'discovery' of the islands to the 20th century.

Williams, E, *From Columbus to Castro: The History of the Caribbean 1492-1969* (1983), André Deutsch. An economic history of the colonial period and slavery, with the rise and fall of the sugar industry.

Economy, politics and society

Ferguson, J, *Dominican Republic, Beyond the Lighthouse* (1992), Latin America Bureau (Research and Action) Ltd. Taking the Faro a Colón as the symbol of the great divide between rich and poor, the social, economic and political crises of the 1990s are explored.

Howard, D, *Dominican Republic in focus: a guide to the people, politics and culture* (1999), Latin America Bureau (Research and Action) Ltd, in the UK and Interlink Books, in the USA. An excellent introduction to the country, one of the best in the In Focus series.

Pattullo, P, *Last Resorts, The Cost of Tourism in the Caribbean* (1996), Cassell in association with Latin America Bureau (paperback LAB 2003). A critical analysis of the tourist industry and the exploitative effect it has on the islands in the Caribbean, including the Dominican Republic.

Travelogue

Crewe, Q, *Touch the Happy Isles: A Journey Through the Caribbean* (1987), Michael Joseph. An affectionate yet perceptive account of travels through the Dominican Republic during his peregrination around the Caribbean.

Language

Foreign languages, particularly English, are spoken in most tourist resorts. However, if you are planning to travel off the beaten track, a working knowledge of Spanish is essential.

General pronunciation

Whether you have been taught the 'Castillian' pronunciation (*z* and *c* followed by *i* or *e* are prounounced as *th* in think) or the 'American' pronunciation (they are pronounced as *s*), you will encounter little difficulty in understanding either. Regional accents and usages vary, but the basic language is essentially the same everywhere.

Vowels

a: as in 'cat'
i: as in 'feet'
u: as in 'food'
ei: as in 'they'

e: as in 'best'
o: as in 'shop'
ai: as in 'ride'
oi: as in 'toy'

Consonants

Most cononants can be prounounced more or less as they are in English. The exceptions are:

g: before *e* and *i* it is the same as **j** (see below)

h: is always silent (except in *ch* as in chair)

j: as the *ch* in Scottish 'loch'

ll: as the *y* in 'yellow'

ñ: as the *ni* in 'onion'

rr: trilled much more than in English

x: depending on its location, pronounced *x, s, sh or j*

Basics

Thank you (very much) *(muchas) gracias*

please *por favor*

hi *hola*

good morning *buenos días*

good afternoon/evening/night *buenas tardes, noches*

goodbye *adiós/chao*

excuse me/I beg your pardon *con permiso*

yes/no *sí/no*

Numbers

one *uno/una*, two *dos*, three *tres*, four *cuatro*, five *cinco*, six *seis*, seven *siete*, eight *ocho*, nine *nuevo*, 10 *diez*, 11 *once*, 12 *doce*, 13 *trece*, 14 *catorce*, 15 *quince*, 16 *dieciséis*, 17 *diecisiete*, 18 *dieciocho*, 19 *diecineuve*, 20 *veinte*, 21 *veintiuno*, 22 *veintidos*, 30 *treinta*, 40 *cuarenta*, 50 *cincuenta*, 60 *sesenta*, 70 *setenta*, 80 *ochenta*, 90 *noventa*, 100 *cien* or *ciento*, 1000 *mil*.

Days and months

Monday *lunes*, Tuesday *martes*, Wednesday *miércoles*, Thursday *jueves*, Friday *viernes*, Saturday *sábado*, Sunday *domingo*; January *enero*, February *febrero*, March *marzo*, April *abril*, May *mayo*, June *junio*, July *julio*, August *agosto*,

September *septiembre*, October *octubre*, November *noviembre*, December *diciembre*.

Questions

how? *¿cómo?*
how much? *¿cuánto cuesta?*
when? *¿cuándo?*
where is? *¿dónde está?*
why? *¿por qué?*
what? *¿qué?*

Problems

I don't understand *no entiendo*
I don't speak Spanish *no hablo español*
How do you say...(in Spanish)? *¿comó se dice... (en español)?*
Do you speak English? *¿habla usted inglés?*

Getting around

bus *el bus/el autobus/la guagua*
bus station *la terminal*
airport *el aeropuerto*
left/right *izquierda/derecha*
straight on *derecho*
to walk *caminar*
street *la calle*
corner *la esquina*
What time does the bus leave for _? *¿A qué hora sale el bus para _?*
How do I get to _? *¿cómo llego a _?*

Shopping

this one/that one *este/esto*
more/less *más/menos*
cheap/expensive *barato/caro*
Do you have anything cheaper? *¿Tiene algo más barato?*

Accommodation

single/double *sencillo/doble*
a double bed *una cama matrimonial*
bathroom *el baño*
breakfast *el desayuno*
air conditioning *el aire acondicionado*
all-inclusive *todo incluido*
for one night/one week *para una noche/semana*

Eating out

avocado *el aguacate*
beans *los frijoles*
bread *el pan*
the bill *la cuenta*
cheese *el queso*
drink *la bebida*
fish *el pescado*
ham *el jamón*
ice cream *el helado*
meal/food *la comida*
milk *la leche*
onion *la cebolla*
pepper *el pimiento*
pork *el cerdo*
prawns *los camarones*
rice *el arroz*
sandwich *el bocadillo*
seafood *los mariscos*
soup *la sopa*
squid *los calamares*
sweet potato *la batata*
vegetables *los legumbres*
without meat *sin carne*

banana chips *tostones*
beef *la carne de res*
breakfast *el desayuno*
butter *la mantequilla*
chicken *el pollo*
egg *el huevo*
goat *el chivo*
hot, spicy *picante*
lobster *la langosta*
meat *la carne*
omelette *el revolrillo*
orange *la naranja*
plantain *el plátano*
potato *la papa*
raw *crudo*
salad *la ensalada*
sauce *la salsa*
soft drink *el refresco*
squash *la calabaza*
sugar *el azúcar*
turkey *el pavo*
water (mineral) *el agua (mineral)*
yam *el ñame*

Index

Credits

Footprint credits

Editor: Nicola Jones
Map editor: Sarah Sorensen
Picture editor: Robert Lunn

Publisher: Patrick Dawson
Series created by: Rachel Fielding
In-house cartography: Claire Benison,
Kevin Feeney, Robert Lunn, Melissa Lin
Proof-reading: Elizabeth Barrick

Design: Mytton Williams
Maps: Footprint Handbooks Ltd

Photography credits

Front cover: Alamy (vendor in
Boca Chica)
Inside: Alamy, except p5 and p35
Powerstock
Generic images: John Matchett
Back cover: Alamy (humpback whale)

Print

Manufactured in Italy by LegoPrint
Pulp made from sustainable forests

Footprint feedback

We try as hard as we can to make
each Footprint guide as up to date as
possible but, of course, things always
change. If you want to let us know
about your experiences – good, bad
or ugly – then, don't delay, go to
www.footprintbooks.com and send
in your comments.

® Footprint Handbooks and the
Footprint mark are a registered
trademark of Footprint Handbooks Ltd

Publishing information

Footprint Dominican Republic
1st edition
Text and maps
© Footprint Handbooks Ltd
October 2004

ISBN 1 904777 08 2
CIP DATA: a catalogue record for this book
is available from the British Library

Published by Footprint
6 Riverside Court
Lower Bristol Road
Bath, BA2 3DZ, UK
T +44 (0)1225 469141
F +44 (0)1225 469461
discover@footprintbooks.com
www.footprintbooks.com

Distributed in the USA by
Publishers Group West

Publishing stuff

Complete title list

Latin America & Caribbean

Argentina
Barbados (P)
Bolivia
Brazil
Caribbean Islands
Central America & Mexico
Chile
Colombia
Costa Rica
Cuba
Cusco & the Inca Trail
Dominican Republic (P)
Ecuador & Galápagos
Guatemala
Havana (P)
Mexico
Nicaragua
Peru
Rio de Janeiro
South American Handbook
St Lucia (P)
Venezuela

North America

Vancouver (P)
New York (P)
Western Canada

Africa

Cape Town (P)
East Africa
Egypt
Libya
Marrakech (P)
Morocco
Namibia
South Africa
Tunisia
Uganda

Middle East

Dubai (P)
Israel
Jordan
Syria & Lebanon

Asia

Bali
Bangkok & the Beaches
Bhutan
Cambodia
Goa
Hong Kong (P)
India
Indian Himalaya
Indonesia
Laos
Malaysia
Myanmar (Burma)
Nepal
Northern Pakistan
Pakistan
Rajasthan & Gujarat
Singapore
South India
Sri Lanka
Sumatra
Thailand
Tibet
Vietnam

Australasia

Australia
East Coast Australia
New Zealand
Sydney (P)
West Coast Australia

Europe

Andalucía
Barcelona (P)
Berlin (P)
Bilbao (P)
Bologna (P)
Britain
Cardiff (P)
Copenhagen (P)
Croatia
Dublin (P)
Edinburgh (P)
England
Glasgow (P)
Ireland
Lisbon (P)
London
London (P)
Madrid (P)
Naples (P)
Northern Spain
Paris (P)
Reykjavík (P)
Scotland
Scotland Highlands
 & Islands
Seville
Spain
Tallin (P)
Turin (P)
Turkey
Valencia (P)
Verona (P)

Lifestyle

Surfing Europe

(P) denotes pocket guide

248

of the Caribbean

BWIA's A340 has the largest seat and legroom ever, as well as the quietest cabin in the sky.

Cross the atlantic in luxurious comfort and style on our A340. You can enjoy up to a staggering 60" seat pitch in business class and up to a really generous 38" in economy. Add to that our renowned friendly and professional service, it's no wonder we fly more people to the Caribbean than any other.

For more information please call 0870 499 2942 or visit our website at www.bwee.com.

SHARING OUR WARMTH WITH THE WORLD

Map 1 Zona Colonial

Av Mexico

Ramón M. Mella

Iglesia de Santa Bárbara
Fuerte de Santa Bárbara
Fuerte del Anguĺo

Paira Alba

España

Puente Flotant

Fuerte de San Antón
Gral G Puello

Gral Cabral

Fuerte de la Carena
Puerta de las Atarazana

Capilla de San Antón

Av Duarte

Benito González

Jacinto de la Concha

José Reyes

Fuerte de San Francisco

Vicente C Duarte

Museo Naval de las Atarazanas

Batería del Almirante

Museo Mundo de Ambar

Restauración

Colón

La Atarazana

Altagracia

Alcázar de Colón & Museo Virreinal

Av Mella

La Noria

Emilio Tejera

Puerta de San Diego

Fuerte de San Miguell

Ceron

Isidoro Pérez

Monasterio de San Francisco

Plaza España

Fuerte de San Diego

Mercado Modelo
Fuerte de San Lázaro

Restauración

Iglesia de San Miguel

Museo de las Casas Reales

Capilla de Nuestra Señora Los Remedios

Convento de San Ignacio de Loyola/ Fuerte de la Caridad

Santiago Rodríguez

Las Mercedes

Iglesia de la Altagracia

Museo de Ambar

Iglesia de San Lázaro

Hospital-Iglesia de San Nicolás de Bari

Panteón Nacional

Las Damas

Igles n Carlos

Luperón

Fuerte Invencible

Fuerte de la Concepción

Iglesia de las Mercedes

Salomé Ureña

Museo de Hernán Córtes

Casa de Ovando

Av Duarte

Hostos

Arz Merino

Parque Colón

Casa de Don Rodrigo de Bastidas & Museo Infantil

Cruise Ship Terminal

Al del Puerto

Puerta del Conde

El Conde

Catedral Basílica Menor de Santa María

Parque dependencia

Arz Nouel

José Reyes

19 de Marzo

Museo de Larimar

Isabel La Católica

Fuerte de Santiago

Capilla de San Andrés

Iglesia del Carmen

Padre Billini

Museo de la Familia Dominicana

Iglesia Santa Clara

Fortaleza Ozama Fortaleza Santo Domingo

Can

Piña

Palo Hincado

Espaillat

Sánchez

Santomé

Capilla de la Tercera Orden

Convento de los Dominicos

Convento Regina Angelorum

Arz Portés

Puerta de la Misericordia

José Gabriel García

Fuerte de San José

Fuerte de San Gil

Estrella

Paseo Pte Billini

Monumento Fray Antón de Montesinos

N

0 metres   100
0 yards   100

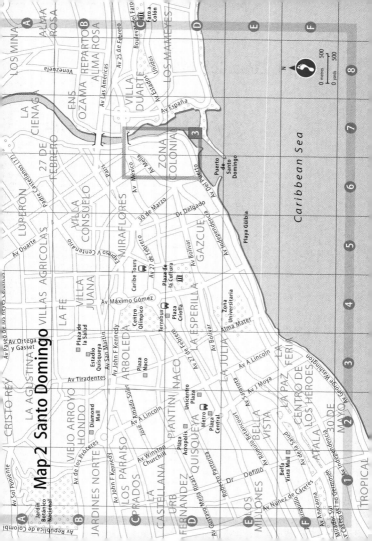

For a different view…
choose a Footprint

Over 100 Footprint travel guides
Covering more than 150 of the world's most exciting
countries and cities in Latin America, the Caribbean, Africa, Indian
sub-continent, Australasia, North America, Southeast Asia, the
Middle East and Europe.

Discover so much more…
The finest writers. In-depth knowledge. Entertaining and accessible.
Critical restaurant and hotels reviews. Lively descriptions of all the
attractions. Get away from the crowds.